NEIL USHER

THE
ELEMENTAL
WORKPLACE

THE 12 ELEMENTS FOR CREATING A FANTASTIC
WORKPLACE FOR EVERYONE

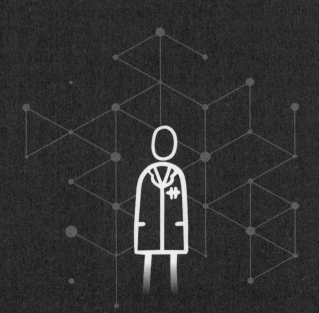

ADVANCE PRAISE

"Starting with the compelling promise that everyone deserves a fantastic workplace, *The Elemental Workplace* sets out to understand how to design workplaces that suit people and organizations. The complexities of workplace design are unpacked and organized into 12 Elements including an easy to follow set of guidelines and metrics. Neil Usher's book is timely and urgently needed. In an industry where buzzwords are too common and myths abound, this book is based on evidence but at the same time down to earth and practical. And funny. A must-read for anyone interested in how to make workplaces work. And that should be all of us."

Dr Kerstin Sailer
Reader in Social and Spatial Networks, Space Syntax Laboratory,
The Bartlett School of Architecture, University College London (UCL)

"This is *the* handbook for anyone asked to oversee an office design for the first time. It is a clear, comprehensive and thoughtful guide, and the reader will benefit hugely from Neil's vast experience in this field. With a liberal sprinkling of philosophy and poetry (for which he is renowned), Neil applies the same level of scrutiny to high level strategic questions as to the tactical details, giving the reader the benefit of his wisdom and practical experience. Regardless of budget, this is essential reading for anyone tasked with 'the office move'. If there was a degree in 'Workplace' this would be the textbook."

Gill Parker
CEO, BDG architecture + design

"Neil has produced an informative, witty handbook for creating a great place to work. Keep it close at hand when the consultants come visiting."

Andrew Brown
Built environment PR consultant

"Paradoxically, as technology automates much of the work we do, the workplace has never been more important. Today, though, it has to provide a space that enables us to make the most of the human skills that set us apart from the machines. *The Elemental Workplace* brilliantly explains what is needed to make this happen. By focusing on 12 'Elements' that are common to all successful workplaces, and then defining both why they matter and how to get them right, this book provides you with a framework to create the space that is right for your company. Each workplace is different, but the good ones are all built on the same foundations. This book will make you think about what matters, what is indeed Elemental."

Antony Slumbers
Innovation in Real Estate, People, Product and #PropTech

"*The Elemental Workplace* sounded (characteristically for Neil Usher) intriguing. Neil has a turn of phrase that is poetic and ahead of the times. This makes his work appeal even more to me. Art always precedes science, business and the rest. So, is Neil an artist? In my view, yes. Is the concept and this book an artform? It is. Like Punk, Hip-Hop and Jazz are to music. Not manufactured and faux. Designed and emergent. Of the people, for the people. If you want to know how to find, build, convert and set up the most human and productive of workplaces, you can find what you need in this book. Space; pace and face. Neil's writing helps you put the smile into all three."

Perry Timms
Founder and Chief Energy Officer,
People and Transformational HR Ltd

Published by
LID Publishing Limited
The Record Hall, Studio 204,
16-16a Baldwins Gardens,
London EC1N 7RJ, UK

524 Broadway, 11th Floor, Suite 08-120,
New York, NY 10012, US

info@lidpublishing.com
www.lidpublishing.com

A member of:

BPR
Business Publishers Roundtable

www.businesspublishersroundtable.com

© Neil Usher, 2018
© LID Publishing Limited, 2018

Printed in Great Britain by TJ International
ISBN: 978-1-911498-64-3

Cover and page design: Matthew Renaudin

NEIL USHER

THE ELEMENTAL WORKPLACE

THE 12 ELEMENTS FOR CREATING A FANTASTIC WORKPLACE FOR EVERYONE

LONDON   MONTERREY
MADRID   SHANGHAI
MEXICO CITY   BOGOTA
NEW YORK   BUENOS AIRES
BARCELONA   SAN FRANCISCO

CONTENTS

ACKNOWLEDGEMENTS

In more than 25 years in the property and workplace profession, I have met and worked with a number of inspiring and extremely helpful people, many of whom may find recollections in this book of ideas upon which we have agreed, disagreed and agreed to disagree. Some have written extensively about the subject and thereby contributed to this book, some have been employed within the profession, and some have had nothing to do with it at all but have offered unique insights from a different angle altogether. Some I have yet to meet face to face, but their thinking, generosity and encouragement online warrant my gratitude.

In no particular order, therefore, I would like to sincerely thank: Antony Slumbers, Nigel Oseland, Ian Ellison, Doug Shaw, Kerstin Sailer, Mark Catchlove, Paul Carder, Sara Bean, Mark Eltringham, Lloyd Davis, Brian Condon, Anke Holst, Simon Heath, Neil Webster, Tony Hall, Laurie Aznavoorian, Gareth Jones, Gemma Dale, Julie Drybrough, Craig Knight, David D'Souza, Ana Stanojevic, Shawn Callahan, Mark McKergow, Kursty Groves, Philip Ross, Stephen Cox, Euan Semple, Jeremy Myerson, Chris Kane, Felicity Roocke, Kate Griffiths-Lambeth, Liz Kentish, Colin Stuart, Polly Plunket-Checkemian, Tim Oldman, Juliette Morgan, Mervyn Dinnen, Perry Timms, Phil Wilcox, Gill Parker, Janet Parkinson, Steve Maslin, Stephen Toft, Luke Fleming, Mark Simpson, Jason Turner, Victoria Ward, Khurshed Dehnugara, Luis Suárez, Philip Tidd, Mark Tittle, Richard Buckley, Paige Hodsman, Rex Barnes, Sarah Lewis, Marie Puybaraud, Andrew Talbot, Steve Coster, Conor Moss, Ziona Strelitz, Nick Green, Anne Marie Rattray, Richard Evans, Andrew Brown, Roger Reeves, Martin Pickard, Monica Parker, Richard Martin, Valerie Valdez, Andrew Mawson, Andy Swann, Will Elgood, Mindy Glover, Martin Christie and Wayne Spiller.

If I have missed you off this list, my apologies; I would be delighted to be told.

FOREWORD

JEREMY MYERSON

For people with long memories in the workplace industry who have witnessed restless waves of change over several decades, it is sometimes hard to believe that the modern office is less than 150 years old.

So prolific and so insistent has been the production and sharing of new workplace concepts – each new format reversing the ideology of the ones preceding it – that it can be hard to know exactly where we stand in designing workplaces in which people can perform to the best of their abilities and even enjoy the experience.

The truth is that the global workplace industry has long been addicted to finding the 'magic bullet' that will reconcile the inevitable contradictions of office design – between the aims of the organization and the needs of the individual, between a fixed architecture of infrastructure and systems and the more flexible patterns of occupation addressed by interior design, between the efficiency of the machine and the creativity of the human.

When the influential US management thinker Thomas Davenport recently reviewed a wide variety of office schemes for knowledge workers, he concluded that there had been considerable investment and experimentation to learn not a lot. Most projects, he observed, were based on "fad, fashion and faith".[1]

This "desperate search for the Holy Grail", as Neil Usher describes it in *The Elemental Workplace*, has resulted in an over-elaboration of planning and designing for the workplaces of the early 21st century. What should be simple and achievable has become difficult and complex.

Neil's intervention with this book is therefore timely and

---

1   T.H, Davenport, R.J. Thomas and S. Cantrell, "The Mysterious Art and Science of Knowledge-Worker Performance," *MIT Sloan Management Review* Fall (2002): p23-30.

important given its aim to demystify the subject, break it down to the essentials and disentangle workplace design from arguments about aesthetics and style.

One of the most damaging developments in recent years has been the aestheticizing of workplace concepts such as collaboration and interaction, creating new environments based on the flimsiest of evidence that they actually work. The power of architectural photography to help design firms win clients, and help clients win over employees, has been instrumental in generating a growing obsession with workstyle.

You will note that this publication has been freed from the tyranny of the architectural photograph. Neil doesn't want the 'look' of real case studies to interfere with the underlying fundamentals he needs to discuss. *The Elemental Workplace* is therefore sparse and pared down in approach, all the better to address the essentials of workplace design, which are presented here for clarity almost like a Periodic Table.

Don't confuse the crystalline form with a rigidly dogmatic line, however. Neil made his name working on big projects in facilities management by adopting an open, intelligent, non-partisan approach.

When I reviewed his scheme for Sky Central in London, which emphatically avoided putting staff through a change management programme and concentrated on providing great spaces for people to explore and adopt in their own way, I commented that it marked the rise of the "non-doctrinaire workplace".

Neil takes a similarly non-doctrinaire approach in this book. He is both poet and pragmatist: on the one hand, he accepts that modern offices "scream for inspiration" and, on the other hand, he provides a wealth of practical, down-to-earth, actionable advice without over-egging his angle on the subject.

The components of his Elemental Workplace include working for everyone ("fully inclusive"), doing your best for staff within inevitable constraints ("sufficiently spacious"), flooding space with daylight and giving the individual local control over the environment. Stimulation and comfort are key ingredients of his package to banish the mediocre.

We say hurrah to all this because treating the organization like a giant piece of engineering that only needs its bolts tightening with a productivity push no longer works. Any recent knowledge of the workplace tells us that culture, experience and wellbeing must come before any efficiency drive.

I recently attended a lecture by Dieter Jäger, formerly managing partner of the Quickborner team in Germany and a pioneer of *Bürolandschaft*, one of the most enduring new formats in workplace design over the past 60 years. Jäger explained how America fell for *Bürolandschaft* in the 1960s and 1970s in a big way. But he was quick to set past achievements in a contemporary frame of concern: "The problem was always to convince organizations that they needed to be reformed before we put them in a new landscape."

Jäger's comments hold a resonance for readers of *The Elemental Workplace*. Neil has entertainingly set out a series of shrewd steps to design and deliver a desirable new landscape for work. Will companies reform their thinking enough to adopt these ideas? I very much hope so and, as a daylight-flooded optimist, I believe they will.

Jeremy Myerson
Helen Hamlyn Professor of Design, Royal College of Art, Director of WORKTECH Academy

This book is for my three loves: Kate, Ava and Mae

THE ELEMENTAL WORKPLACE:

A fully inclusive, sufficiently spacious, stimulating and daylight-flooded workplace, providing super-connectivity and localized environmental control, while allowing individual influence over a choice of comfortable, considered settings, offering convenient and secure storage for personal and business effects, affordable and healthy refreshments, and clean, well-stocked washrooms.

Everyone deserves a fantastic workplace.
This guide tells you in a simple, easy-to-follow way why you need a fantastic workplace, how to create it and what it comprises.

#elementalworkplace

PART ONE

WHY

RIDICULOUS
BEGINNINGS

*"All great deeds and all great thoughts
have a ridiculous beginning."*
Albert Camus, *The Myth of Sisyphus*[2]

A RIDICULOUS IDEA

Everyone deserves a fantastic workplace in which to live, learn, grow, share and contribute. Its creation ought to be intuitive and simple. However, most workplaces silently scream for inspiration and investment, imagination and practical thinking. The propensity to complicate and procrastinate, rather than act, condemns millions the world over to tolerate needless mediocrity. All we need do is cut through the impossible knot. It does not need a paradigm shift, a complex solution, blue-sky thinking or yet another research report – it needs the application of energy, belief and simple sense. We know that a great workplace is motivating and uplifting and contributes to our sense of self-worth and wellbeing, and therefore benefits the organization in which we are employed. It is a ridiculously simple idea, ridiculously easy to implement where there is a willingness to do so.

The roots of *The Elemental Workplace* can be traced back to a blog post I wrote in October 2012: "A Tale of Two Cities: The Workplace Poverty Index[3]". I saw that a small clutch of well-funded organizations seemed to be spinning away from the mass of unexceptional ones at an increasingly faster rate,

---

2   Albert Camus, *The Myth of Sisyphus*, trans. Justin O'Brien (London: Penguin, 1975).

3   Neil Usher, "A Tale of Two Cities: the Workplace Poverty Index," *Workessence*, October 9, 2012, http://workessence.com/a-tale-of-two-cities-the-workplace-poverty-index/

their superior status reinforced at glitzy events. This was frustrating for those left behind, yet I could see that there were some easy, low-cost things that could be done to improve the workplace.

Shortly afterwards, in November 2012, the emotion clearly still bubbling, I wrote a post called "Ministry of the Bleeding Obvious"[4] where I further pursued the idea that improving the workplace substantially was far from difficult if we focused on the right things. It stressed that we already have the understanding and resources needed to do something about it.

The post that gave voice to the whole idea was published on 29 June 2014,[5] originally called "The Living Wage Workplace" but changed very soon after to "The Elemental Workplace". It outlined ten (as there were then) 'Elements': daylight, connectivity, space, choice, influence, control, refresh, sense, wash and storage. It was presented and tested through participative forums with people from a variety of backgrounds, and the ten eventually became 12 when I realized I was missing a couple: comfort and inclusion. The Human Resources (HR) community proved particularly engaged with the idea. It has appeared since in various guises through a number of posts, but the limitations of blogging in terms of diminished attention span persuaded me that, three years later, it was time to explain myself more fully.

The idea has two pillars. First, creating a fantastic workplace is simple. That is not to say that we can afford to be simplistic, but that the goal is understandable and practicable. I hope that a sense of optimism prevails as you explore the Elements. We generally refer to 'common sense' a great deal, which seems odd in that such incisive thinking is rarely common – yet it is simple. You will therefore hear me refer to 'simple sense' instead.

Secondly, a fantastic workplace is attainable. The only thing that stands between us and a fantastic workplace is our collective apprehension. Even where money is scarce, ideas on the right way to organize space can conflict or the core business of the organization may allow little time to focus on anything else, but there are ways around the roadblocks when an elemental approach is adopted. It is rarely about gimmicks or mimicking those for whom publicity flows – it is about doing what works for you and your colleagues, having a positive attitude and setting aside the plentiful reasons 'why not'. An 'agile' approach can also help in this regard: a focused team taking small steps that are regularly reviewed. Whichever route is taken, it starts with belief and then follows with a bit of organization.

A RIDICULOUS ADVENTURE

How I arrived here has all been one huge happy accident. I have been there, done it, and am still doing it: 25 years and counting as a property and workplace professional that was never supposed to happen. I had completed a master's degree in Information Technology in 1991, when the Apple Classic was breaking the stale mould of orange letters on a black screen. I had been intent on pursuing life as a 'hybrid manager', a commercially enabled leader who knew the language of IT, who could talk to the geeks

---

4   Neil Usher, "Ministry of the Bleeding Obvious," *Workessence*, November 23, 2012, http://workessence.com/ministry-of-the-bleeding-obvious/

5   Neil Usher, "The Elemental Workplace," *Workessence*, June 29, 2014, http://workessence.com/the-elemental-workplace/

who were in some darkened corners readying themselves to inherit the planet and potentially those beyond. I watched in awe as a fellow student sent an email to her friend at another university. I wrote dark and despairing poetry about dilution of the essence of humanity and the disintegration of social infrastructure from the unstoppable march of the binary. Yet I was nudged from my only three months as a systems analyst into becoming a facilities manager, entering an emerging profession that had only just agreed on a name (strangely, it still has not agreed on a purpose, even to this day).

I always knew something was wrong with the conditions in which we worked. My earliest full-time incarnation in an office was in the spiritual desolation of Marsham Towers (1971-2003), in the heart of Westminster. The vacuum therein was so beautifully captured in a poem I later discovered called "Dolor" by Theodore Roethke[6] (1908-1963), it could have been written about those very threadbare and barren floors:

I have known the inexorable sadness of pencils,
Neat in their boxes, dolor of pad and paper weight,
All the misery of manila folders and mucilage,
Desolation in immaculate public places,
Lonely reception room, lavatory, switchboard,
The unalterable pathos of basin and pitcher,
Ritual of multigraph, paper-clip, comma,
Endless duplication of lives and objects.
And I have seen dust from the walls of institutions,
Finer than flour, alive, more dangerous than silica,
Sift, almost invisible, through long afternoons of tedium,
Dropping a fine film on nails and delicate eyebrows,
Glazing the pale hair, the duplicate grey standard faces.

What struck me most was the resigned spirit of those encased in these gloomy institutions, strumming at the tedium, carving a life that didn't matter around the regular arrival of work in neatly stuffed transit envelopes without which the world might slow on its axis. There was so much that could have been done to add energy, yet that "fine film" of dust had settled at a level unable to ignite concern. It left just about enough energy for the work to carry on.

How delighted I was, therefore, to find a role in which I could do something to redress the deceleration. It took me, by opportune yet unplanned steps, through a series of increasingly broader corporate roles, managing property strategy, transactions, development, workplace creation and operational services with the likes of PolyGram, Warner Bros., Honeywell, Rio Tinto and Sky. All the way back to the sadness of those pencils, being able to see and touch the product of my efforts has been a factor that has kept me in the profession when at times the challenges and frustrations might otherwise have taken me on a different path. I do not plan on doing anything else – this is my course.

By 2010 it was a liberating surprise to find that my master's-era reflections had been wrong, that technology had created the possibility of exponential social growth. From my first Twitter account in 2009, and inspired by some marvellous people at the Tuttle Club – a gathering every Friday morning at the (sadly now closed) Centre for Creative Collaboration (C4CC) in London's Kings Cross – I started to "write myself into existence",

---

6   "Dolor," copyright © 1943 by Modern Poetry Association, Inc. Copyright © 1966 and renewed 1994 by Beatrice Lushington; from COLLECTED POEMS by Theodore Roethke. Used by permission of Doubleday, an imprint of the Knopf Doubleday Publishing Group, a division of Penguin Random House LLC. All rights reserved.

as David Weinberger said in *The Cluetrain Manifesto*,[7] combining the short (Twitter) and long (blog) forms. I set up a free blog site on the now-defunct Posterous platform in 2010 and then, when I had managed to draw in a small but committed readership, I created the *Workessence* site (www.workessence.com). All the posts are still there. At last I had a platform to share my internal struggles about work, the workplace, social business and people-centred issues – and a place to give airtime to a ridiculous idea.

A colleague recently described the *Workessence* blog as "One of the best out there by far – in terms of insight, breadth, voice, awareness, perspective. But it is undeniably contrary, can be cantankerous, seeks to provoke and some might suggest rather anti-establishment." A blog must have an edge, possibly even serrated, whereas a book needs to have a purpose. I am rather hoping that I have transferred some of the spirit and energy of the blogging adventure and the learning from a corporate trek through various industries clutching a round-the-world plane ticket into what is ultimately intended to be a practical guide.

Roethke's poem has never left me; the dust still falls. We know that with a little leadership and conviction, we can make the Elemental Workplace happen. We can do this, we have to do this, and I really do believe we will.

THIS RIDICULOUS BOOK

It is worth explaining the purpose and scope of the book. In terms of scope, the workplace – by which I mean the office, the factory of this century and the last – may be a large corporate building that forms part of a national or international network, a space in which the whole organization resides, or a space shared by many smaller organizations or individuals 'co-working'. It may be anywhere in the world, be private or public or even its own sector, and may support any one of an increasing variety of organizational structures.

The book is intended for everyone, whether managing a property portfolio or a project, owning or running a business, or just interested in the workplace to which they are treated, or subject. It has had the corporate bullshit and buzzwords surgically removed. It is not a 'business book' – it is equally not a disruptor, and introduces only a simple, bite-sized and easily digestible concept. As long as physical workspace is required, this book will remain relevant. The Elements will apply, however automated our lives and buildings become – or, at least, until delivering on the contents of this book becomes automatic. It is also not a niche book for the workplace professionals. While some parts or ideas may seem obvious to those within the discipline, most organizations have someone responsible for the workplace, yet a lot of work still needs to be done.

The book is not, like many in the field, a travelogue decked out with rafts of enviable pictures of just-completed workspaces occupied by a few friends of the architectural photographer; it is independent of the aesthetic outcome. It deals with the components of the space and how they relate to one another and function, not how they might look. There is still a significant role for the Brief (with an initial capital, given its importance – more on this later),

---

7   Rick Levine, Christopher Locke, Doc Searls, David Weinberger et al., *The Cluetrain Manifesto*, Tenth Anniversary Edition (New York: Basic Books, 2011).

for design and for creativity; the book is not intended to replace any of these contributions. It is also independent of the intended workstyle, whether it be enclosed, open, flexible, agile, hybrid or whatever term is used to describe the intention. It works for them all.

Many of the threads, ideas and fragments in this book have been used and deployed by others, as is now common in a world of more open and shared intellectual property. However, what often happens in the rush to create a model or a robust list is that, after a promising start, ideas tend to give way to specifics rather than holding to a consistent and evenly weighted framework. Such treatments have also tended to pivot on a point of expertise, a service, product or recent project, creating a degree of substance around the core theme to support it, but little more. They run out of breath and conviction very quickly.

This book attempts to be even in its treatment of the 12 Elements. Stefan Zweig once stated that "The elemental will always conquer the ephemeral."[8] Yet the ephemeral, or temporary, often commands undue attention and consumes a great deal of the available cash. These features often create significant enthusiasm – but enthusiasm rarely lasts long. Goethe compared it to an oyster,[9] needing to be consumed while fresh. The ephemeral – those aspects whose appeal lasts for a very short time – can be dealt with in due course. They do have a relevance, but they should not be the main focus, or a glittering distraction. They warrant a short chapter, much later.

There are no case studies to be found in the book, due to the difficulty of extracting impartial information. Such studies also inevitably demand images and, as explained, I have tried to steer clear of the tendency to sprinkle the text with distractions. Nor are there interviews with other practitioners and consultants, as these can confuse the picture with the clamour of too many competing voices. Case studies and interviews also present the problem of date-stamping a text that I hope will stand the test of time. It is better to seek out case studies and perspectives of your own, not those I have forced upon you.

I have read and absorbed countless research reports and written and spoken perspectives on the subject throughout my career. I have referenced those quoted and specifically mentioned in the book, and provided a number that may be helpful in the Resources section at the end. Unfortunately, the sources of some remain unidentified. Yet this is not an academic work. I have also avoided lists and bullet points, as they do not feel appropriate to the weaving of stories. I like the idea of this book being a paper copy, dog-eared, scribbled on, notes in the margins, falling apart, the equivalent of being released on vinyl, with a gatefold sleeve rich in notes.

A RIDICULOUS DISCIPLINE

The contribution that the workplace might make for the individual and collective benefit of people and the organizations for whom they work is at last being recognized, albeit far from universally. Standards of workplace design, creation and management are beginning to improve for the fortunate few, yet the majority (particularly beyond

8   Stefan Zweig, *Shooting Stars: Ten Historical Miniatures* (London: Pushkin Press, 2015) p114.

9   Johann Wolfgang Goethe, *Gedichte: Ausgabe Letzter Hand 1927* (Berlin: Hofenberg, 2016).

first-tier city centres) remain dull, unimaginative and uninspiring, ill-equipped, poorly maintained, playing to a misguided idea of what 'corporate' should represent, and supportive and reflective of archaic management practices.

Meanwhile the workplace sector – by which I mean all those associated with workplace strategy, analysis, design and construction – is only beginning to find and understand itself, and gear itself up for the challenge. 'Workplace' is an immature and vulnerable discipline composed of minor yet far more mature disciplines. It is a composite like most (there are few that are pure), but a discipline in its own right nevertheless.

On the positive side, it is enthusiastic in view of the shards of light penetrating the apathy, and has something of the emergent spirit that facilities management (FM) possessed in the early 1990s, before it rather underplayed the opportunity afforded by its scale, scope and existing critical mass. The same must not happen here.

Yet it is still long on shortcomings. It is uncoordinated and unrepresented, quick to cry 'problem' but inarticulate in its response, with an unfortunate habit of talking to itself. It is defective in client-side skills, though well set up for point-professional expertise such as design, project and cost management; it is socially disconnected in that it rarely effectively networks with related functions, and hence overall it lacks identity, confidence and cohesion. Appeals, such as those originated by Paul Carder[10] in a blog post and repeated in the *Stoddart Review*[11] (a not-for-profit initiative co-ordinated by several organizations in 2016 that resulted in the *Workplace Advantage* report), for a 'chief workplace officer' to draw together activities associated with property, HR and technology (among others) under a singular role are interesting but premature; firmer foundations are needed.

Finally, workplace struggles in its relationship with an intrinsically related discipline that sits at something akin to the last frontier: change. There is a simple remedy based on a fundamental principle that is rarely understood: the journey to a fantastic workplace is a change journey. It flips prevailing practice 180 degrees. 'Change management' is not a downstream plug-in to a workplace project; rather the workplace project is a downstream plug-in to a change journey that began with the first twinkle in the eye (or perhaps on perusing this book...) and will continue long after the builders, installers, technicians, consultants and movers have all settled their final accounts and moved on. More on this in the later chapter "Rivers of change".

There is every cause for optimism; the beginnings of a discipline can be directed towards growth, identity and self-awareness. This book is intended to give some impetus to the discipline through creating the belief that progress can be made simply and easily. As outlined below, we first need to shed some unnecessary baggage.

RIDICULOUS MYTHS

Despite some progress, the field continues to suffer from a desperate search for the Holy Grail, the one idea that will save us all. It 'penduluminates' (my word) – taking an idea, shining a bright light upon it and then pushing it to

---

10   Paul Carder, "Where Should the 'Director of Work' Fit into Large Organizations?" *The Occupier's Journal*, August 9, 2012, http://occupiersjournal.com/ where-should-the-director-of-work-fit-into-large-organisations/

11   *The Workplace Advantage: The Stoddart Review* (London: Raconteur Custom Publishing, 2016).

the extreme until its energy is exhausted, before letting it swing all the way back whence it started. It is a field that is awash with well-intentioned data that is essentially empty, supporting whatever thesis is desired through immature definition and interpretation. Trapped in these amalgamated responses are the disgruntled voices of thousands of people unable to tell us just why they are unhappy with where they work, or what might be done about it. Yet, most of all, it struggles with a horror that the simple path may be the right path. It gets wrapped up in thought, obstructing progress. In doing so it allows repetition to create a version of truth: if we say it and hear it enough times, it must be the case. In this manner, excellent observations such as "Work is something you do, not somewhere you go" become gnarled, twisted and ugly representations of the original gem of inspiration.

A number of myths therefore persist. In each there may be some grain of truth, or subtlety of insight, but they are at once a state of affairs that is clouding our ability to act, and ideas that will not find fruit in this book. They are about to be summarily despatched.

Work is indeed something we do, yet it is also a place we go *and* a product we create. It is a many-faceted idea that needs to be considered in the fullest sense. Yet, while it has become increasingly important to understand that we can set people free from the routine fetters of the desk and trust them to be productive – managing them to manage themselves – to entirely discard the idea of a destination space in which we meet to work together is preposterous. The benefit lies not in one replacing the other, but in the combination of the two.

In this sense, therefore, the office is not dead. While it was hoped a couple of decades ago that technology would rid us of the constraints of time and distance, enabling us to work wherever we laid our hat, that has not happened. In many areas, the need for people to physically be together has never been greater – ironically so, in the discipline of 'Agile Engineering' where the technically gifted are creating much of this technology. (This term, coined in the late 1990s, refers to the method of software engineering that involves small iterations of work, regularly checked and validated through team interaction.) Yet technology still allows us the benefit of taking time to work elsewhere too. The rise of co-working has, in turn, underlined the need for individuals or small and medium-sized enterprises to physically locate together for essential human interaction, calling into question the belief that they can be effective on an entirely virtual level. Some small organizations such as Automatic (which created the website management system WordPress) have managed it,[12] but they remain rare. What has actually occurred is that technology has enhanced our ability to physically relate and interact.

The 'robots' are therefore not coming to cast us all into serfdom. Enough technology already exists today to remove a significant percentage of 'white collar' roles, were it to be applied. Artificial intelligence (AI) and its related disciplines will certainly continue to automate where costs can be reduced and accuracy increased – such as abstracting leases in multiple languages, for example – but new roles and new purpose will emerge in their place. Technologies have threatened societal stability before and they will do

---

12 Glenn Leibowitz, "This CEO Runs a Billion-Dollar Company with No Offices or Email," *Inc.com*, March 16, 2016, https://www.inc.com/glenn-leibowitz/meet-the-ceo-running-a-billion-dollar-company-with-no-offices-or-email.html

so again, yet we have a resilience and adaptability that will see us through. We are adept at continually creating new needs.

Among those who are still very much at labour in the workplace, the younger generations still loosely termed 'millennials' (an expression nauseating even to them) are not a breed apart, with an entirely different philosophy of life and a list of picky requirements. The generational differences myth has been so misunderstood, poorly researched and overplayed, that it is disturbing in its triviality. There will be sensitivities to the needs of the young – just as there are with those of the less publicized ageing populations of most industrialized countries – but this does not constitute a model for action, policy or workplace design. We think of everyone, as shall be explored later.

Finally, as concerns the scope of this section, we are not living in an era of unprecedented change. There have been far greater seismic societal shifts in the history of mankind than the technological changes of the past 30 years. It has been argued by economist Ha-Joon Chang[13] and others that the domestic washing machine has created more significant change than any recent invention, including even the internet, freeing women to work and build careers like no other device before it, or since. We *are* living in an era of rapid change but, in relative terms, we always have been. The essential difference is that we perceive the pace of change to be unprecedented now because its coverage is unprecedented. We track change by the fraction of a second, with every post and tweet. Previous societal, demographic and technological shifts were only recognized as such when later historians analysed and explained what had really happened. The fact that we can see change happening does not make it more significant.

Freed of the weight of some of these assumptions, we can now move on and leave others to wrestle them to a stalemate.

From this point on, the first person disappears save for encompassing you, me and all of us – or for the offer of a 'thank you'. It has been necessary to explain a few things, and hopefully we have created a connection. From here, we are looking at the workplace together, from the same standpoint. If you should use this book as a guide to create a new workplace, please do let me know (you can reach me at neilusher@hotmail.com), as I would love to come and see it and hear your story. Thank you for buying the book, and the very best of luck on your change journey.

---

13   Ha-Joon Chang, *23 Things That They Don't Tell You About Capitalism* (London: Penguin, 2011).

WHY CREATE A FANTASTIC WORKPLACE?

The simplest of questions often prompt those moments in which we freeze in time, having progressed along a path only to look around and find our first steps being eroded. Why anyone needs to have a fantastic workplace is just such a question. Away from the co-working start-up comfort of many of today's fledgling businesses, a number of challenger organizations who became mighty were born under considerable adversity. They created their success despite the space in which they operated, not because of it (be careful, however, with the legend of Apple starting in a garage). In some instances, a collective fear of losing that dogged spirit and defiance relegates workplace to a negligible consideration. Hence the question, and the doubt. There is a chapter of the book *Parkinson's Law* dedicated to the workplace, in which it is observed that "a perfection of planned layout is achieved only by institutions on the point of collapse"[14] while dynamic firms are likely to make do and improvise.

Nevertheless, there remains a compelling case for a fantastic workplace that needs to find its voice. To help explain this I have used an enhanced and updated version of the long-standing framework created by Frank Duffy[15] of the architectural practice DEGW (1971-2009), the three 'e's (efficiency, effectiveness, and expression), and made it six (adding environment, ether, and energy). These all add up to creating a workplace that enables the wellbeing, performance and productivity of the occupants, thereby in turn making a significant contribution to the wellbeing, performance and productivity of the organization.

14   C. Northcote Parkinson, *Parkinson's Law* (London: Houghton Mifflin, 1957), p60.

15   Frank Duffy, "Building Appraisal: A Personal View," *Journal of Building Appraisal*, Vol. 4 No. 3 (2009), p149-156.

This book holds that each of the six 'e's is of equal importance, but acknowledges that the balance may shift under certain conditions or in particular industries. First, though, a few thoughts on a dominant concern of our time.

THE PRODUCTIVITY UNICORN

The simple proposition frequently offered in justification of creating a fantastic workplace is that it can (or as is often confidently stated *will*) improve individual and organizational productivity, and can (will) generate a return on investment. Yet it puzzles, beguiles and infuriates us in equal measure as we struggle to agree on a definition, and struggle even more to confidently prove the claim. It is like a mythical beast with magical powers.

There are two types of productivity: the objective (how productive I actually am, by whatever measure is agreed upon) and the subjective (how productive I feel that I am). They are rarely aligned.

My own personal view of my productivity may relate to how many emails I have answered, the number of unnecessary meetings avoided and how much uninterrupted online shopping I have completed, because I set the measure and manage my own conscience. Teamwork just gets in the way. My contribution to organizational productivity may be very low as a result. Of course, I could also be doing some sterling work while hidden away, uninterrupted, and contributing handsomely to organizational productivity.

Conversely, the leaders of most organizations often strive for ways to get their people to work more effectively together, believing that collaborative practices will drive the innovation and progress they are seeking.

Individual work just gets in the way, unless it is in support of group activity. Of course, I could be part of a dysfunctional group without purpose or direction, wasting everyone's time and achieving nothing. I could also be using the smokescreen of group work to avoid getting on with anything productive on my own, and to justify why I haven't been able to do so.

The dual notion of productivity therefore presents a challenge in thinking about the workplace, and necessitates a great degree of care when talking about it.

It is no surprise to find that the workplace sector has assumed the potential to increase objective productivity as the favourable route to executive prioritization for investment. The Stoddart Review's *Workplace Advantage* report is the latest to do so.[16] At least here, the idea of a beneficial return on investment (ROI) has been based on the potential ability of a comparatively small investment in property to generate a significant boost in the productivity of the organization's main investment, its people. We will look at this more specifically below, when we consider efficiency.

All of this assumes, of course, that the contribution of the workplace can be separated from other factors – it is still a much-debated matter, given the difficulties of the challenge. We are also bogged down by the struggle, common to many support functions, for a seat at the executive table. In a world of opinion surveys, a focus on measurable truth is admirable, provided we do not lose sight of the fact that leadership within organizations is capable of making a decision on the grounds that improving the working lives of its employees is *the right thing to do.*

---

16 *The Workplace Advantage: The Stoddart Review* (London: Raconteur Custom Publishing, 2016).

In many respects, a false claim to ROI is more damaging than a straightforward appeal to decent, people-centric action. Facts need to be facts, or they are just guesswork. Boards do not like guesswork, but they will often back conviction.

Some organizations have created reasonable estimates of the benefit – usually those based in a single or key location where all facets of the business come together to facilitate meaningful measurement. Areas such as income per head and cross-team referrals have been identified as proof of a specific ROI. However, they are still not immune from contamination by the sheer number of internal and external influences on these outcomes. You cannot untangle these.

The Elemental Workplace assumes that its successful implementation contributes to productivity, but cannot quantify this contribution and so does not seek to make a claim. It just knows that happier, more energized people with better facilities to hand will likely work harder and be more committed, and even potentially more innovative. It is the right thing to do; the six 'e's tell us so.

We may also like to discard the whole notion of the 'C-Suite', a term referring to top-level executives, as a target audience with a consistent and unified view. The idea of a collective group safe in a fortified keep only serves to reinforce a position of helplessness. Rarely, however, do executive teams constitute a true team with a common position at all, rife as they often are with rivalries. The workplace industry needs to avoid undervaluing and undermining its own subtle ability to influence thinking and decision-making.

It should also be remembered that it is not just a matter of recognizing the importance of the workplace, but of doing it well. It is staggering how often that gets overlooked. It is possible to invest in a workplace transformation and get it horribly wrong, adversely affecting productivity.

Poor Briefing, lazy design, misdirected change enablement, possibly even ill fortune from external influences or market changes – all can bury the investment in regret. Ideally, we aim to achieve an identifiable increase in both forms of productivity, objective and subjective: people should *feel* productive and *be* productive. Though a fantastic workplace can contribute to both through the six 'e's, as we shall see, it still has to be done well – which is what *The Elemental Workplace* can demonstrate.

ADDRESSING THE SIX 'E'S

EFFICIENCY

Creating a fantastic workplace, when justified and made possible by achieving financial and operating efficiencies, is not wrong: take the opportunity. It is not a matter of principle or ideological purity. Accountants are our friends and, if we are to create a fantastic workplace, we need to be in step with the financial agenda of the organization, and on excellent terms with those who can liberate the cash required. It is amazing how antagonistic some property professionals are towards those in positions of financial responsibility; it's an energy not worth wasting. The ability of workplace over the past two to three decades to be commercial has made much of our progress possible.

Measuring efficiency is relatively easy. There are two categories, with objective measures in each. Cost efficiency is captured as cost per square metre/foot, and cost per person within a defined area. Space efficiency is determined as the occupation density (measured in square metres/feet per person) and space utilization (the percentage of space occupied at any one time, or over a given period).

Costs are both non-discretionary (lease, service charges and non-reclaimable taxes) – usually amounting to approximately 70% of a typical facility cost – or discretionary (services provided by the occupant), comprising the other 30%. Consumption costs such as office supplies, printing and telephony are rarely included in these metrics, as they are not space-related.

These factors need to be set against the relative costs of property occupancy to an organization's total 'non-core' (often termed 'operational') cost base, which usually comprises three broad areas: people, process (technology) and place (property). To garner focus, it is still often said by the property profession that property costs are an organization's 'second largest'. However, the general rule of thumb for non-asset-based organizations is that approximately 85% of the cost base is people, 10% property and 5% information technology infrastructure and kit. On this basis, of the 10% that makes up property costs, the non-discretionary costs of property to an organization are 7% of the overall total and the discretionary only 3%.

Measures taken in the name of workplace efficiency therefore have a proportionately significant opportunity to benefit or negatively affect the 85% of the costs that are being expended on people. An organization's people are not an avoidable inconvenience in the way the cost appears on a spreadsheet – they are the very substance of the business.

Utilization is usually measured as a percentage of desks (or other defined units of space) occupied over a period of time. While electronic detection systems (sensors) have been used effectively in some workplaces, at the time of writing, visual observation still captures a greater depth of data than the binary occupied/unoccupied under sensory measurement; it can register not simply a warm body at a desk but also 'signs of life' (where someone has set up a desk and is using it, thereby preventing others from doing so, but is not present) and the nature of the work being undertaken. Most observations of traditional allocated desk (1:1) workspaces find that somewhere between 40-60% of desks are being used at any one time (person present and signs of life combined) due to natural levels of absence – which may be annual leave, illness or working at other locations, including from home. The 40-60% not in use has therefore formed the basis of shifts from allocated to free-address, shared workspace, with an expectation that some (or, frighteningly, all) of this capacity can be removed and less space occupied overall. It is also generally true that more flexible environments cost less to build, as there is less enclosed infrastructure, such as private offices with their associated mechanical and electrical costs.

Efficiency goals therefore have tended towards the occupation of less space overall, at a higher level of density and utilization, and at a lower cost to establish and run.

The more flexible the space within this new regime, the lower the churn costs of moving people when teams within the business grow, contract and change. It should be noted, however, that not every workplace scheme results in reduced space and greater density, or has this as its aim. Sometimes, where an organization has outgrown its space, the opposite is needed, and therefore what is required is caution in calculating the additional space requirement, the aim being to demonstrate efficiency *pro rata* rather than in absolute terms. Efficiency must be handled with care. It can be an important means of justifying workplace transformation – indeed, it can even ensure that it is self-funding – but this should not be to the detriment of its twin soul, effectiveness. Enough advantage should be gained from efficiency to be helpful, and then it should be taken off the table.

An approach driven by efficiency can also make a cultural contribution through the removal of symbols of hierarchy, real and artificial. The double-aspect corner office, with its obligatory secretarial guardhouse and private lavatory – status 'cymbals' (for they can be loud!) – have no place in an environment in which every square metre counts, and every square metre is counted and recharged. Very often, changes to the workplace were required whenever a managerial grade changed or promotion was awarded, for when the symbols are ingrained they become fiercely coveted and protected. The expectation of the outcome needs to be managed, however, as the ejection of the symbols is unlikely to overthrow the manner in which hierarchy and power operate – they will likely find more subtle forms. It makes a visible contribution, nonetheless, and is often a source of powerful change stories.

EFFECTIVENESS

Effectiveness and efficiency are inseparable twins. It is all very well hitting amazing efficiency targets, such as an aggregated 6 square metres (65 square feet) per person in serried ranks of desks at 80%+ occupancy that are swept of any signs of personal ownership, and with personal storage driven down to half a linear metre (20 inches) per person – but workspace has to *work*. This is obvious, but somehow is not.

We instinctively sense that even a small increase in the effectiveness of the workplace and its technology can have a positive effect on the performance of the organization. Given the 85/10/5 split identified in the previous section, the potential of the 15% to benefit the 85% is huge. To what extent it does so, and in what terms this can be measured, relates to the frustrations associated with the 'productivity unicorn' identified earlier.

By effectiveness we mean a number of things working in harmony, including the ability of people to work alone or together, to find colleagues, to have access to the right technology and systems, to have the right amenities and services available at the right time and in the right place, and for the balance of space to be right. In effect, we mean an Elemental Workplace.

It is therefore essential to balance the efficiency of the workplace with its effectiveness. There will be limits to the effectiveness of a workplace where levels of efficiency are constricted too tightly, or are left to dangle too loosely. However, a certain pressure from efficiency is useful in ensuring that the financiers are on side and that sufficient attention is focused on good design and on imposing an atmosphere of questioning and sound decision-making. It should also be borne in mind that a workplace entirely focused on effectiveness is likely to be highly inefficient and create an entitlement culture. Without that pressure from efficiency, it is doubtful whether the results would be anything other than de-energized and distracting indulgence. The importance of having both efficiency and effectiveness in sync creates a tension that is necessary and healthy. It helps us avoid mediocrity at both ends of the spectrum.

Components of a strategy balancing efficiency and effectiveness can be the same thing expressed in different ways. For example, a programme by an organization to reduce the number of buildings occupied in order to save money can also be expressed as a strategy to co-locate the right people to benefit workflow, innovation and process improvement. The end result is the same. The former is music to the ears of the board; the latter is more likely to garner support from those directly affected as long as the distance is manageable.

An effective workplace can create an environment that promotes transparency and therefore trust. In so many respects, trust is the key to excellent behaviours and outcomes. It has no negative characteristics. It allows people to make behavioural choices that benefit themselves and their colleagues. It should be understood, however, that the workplace alone cannot create trust; there are many other layers, including freedom, respect and permission, that are required to work hand in hand with the physical environment for it to flourish.

An effective workplace is one that is built on the principle of simplicity. Most people are generally too busy to have time to deduce how the workplace is supposed to function, and so it should be evident and obvious. Services and amenities should be available in the right place, taking account of people flow. In this way obstacles to productivity are removed, and access to colleagues is improved. Much is made of the idea of 'serendipitous encounters', a more eloquent description of the old American idea of 'watercooler moments', described as such because for most of the day occupants were cooped up in the sort of cubicle life so beautifully captured in Dilbert cartoons, and gathering for a cup of nature's elixir was blessed relief from the isolation.

It is necessary at this point to expand on the quote from Camus that opened the book: "All great deeds and all great thoughts have a ridiculous beginning. Great works are often born on a street corner or in a restaurant's revolving door." Angela Maiers even coined the phrase 'tactical serendipity' which she describes as "the intersection between structure and spontaneity"[17], a little like the much-talked-about example of Google creating deliberately long queues for its free food so that strangers might talk to one another while waiting. Some have of course taken it all far too far, with biological terms such as cross-pollination, symbiosis and incubation, but we are people, not lichen. An effective workplace offers spaces for interaction, journeys that may intersect, pauses that may be shared; all these things allow for randomness. It is still up to the occupants how much they allow into their day, but our role is not to impose restrictions.

An effective workplace is one that inspires and energizes. There is always room for beauty and surprise, with the caution applied that novelties can wear off very quickly, and therefore, where added, need to be capable of rapid change. Novelty is not wrong *per se*, but letting it go stale until it is derided most certainly is. This can happen in a heartbeat. Oddly, novelties often act as an inhibitor when the intention in deploying them is just the opposite – they create claustrophobia and confinement rather than a sense of opportunity. If no one is on the slide, who is going to use it?

Finally – perhaps the most important point, which is often neglected – an effective workplace is one that can facilitate learning and development. Very often facilities for this type of activity are an afterthought: the rooms are at the rear of the space, plain and unloved – "It's just a training room." What does that say about the value placed on development? A useful experiment in changing attitudes to learning is to have these facilities front and centre, evident and available, of the highest quality. It may just transform the way the organization sees and values learning.

---

17 Angela Maiers, "Tactical Serendipity," *Huffpost*, October 14, 2013,
http://www.huffingtonpost.com/angela-maiers/tactical-serendipity_b_4094961.html.

EXPRESSION

It might be easy to think that the discussion ends there – efficiency and effectiveness, get the balance right, go for a beer. Yet, in an age when the value of an organization increasingly resides in its brand, the need for expression has never been greater. Of course, it is all too easy to do this badly, the organization creating a garish monument to itself to fully explain its latest price increases, while its own employees are overdosed with giddying levels of Pantone immersion and billboarded to oblivion. Most people know where they are and who they work for; they do not need to be constantly reminded in this way.

Expression itself therefore needs to be both efficient and effective. It is part of the workplace design task and should not be an overlaid, disconnected afterthought. Very often the expression of an organization's mission, culture, values and purpose – its DNA – can be woven through the design of the space, the components and their arrangement; through what is deemed important, what is shown and what is not; through the behaviour of those providing services and those occupying the space, through the gentle hum of humanity. Expression goes beyond the shallow, transitory idea of brand-*ing*; it is a whole-life idea.

Its effect can be to create an association and commitment among members of the organization, a unifying influence, and to project a subtle and quiet external confidence and reassurance. It is through association that a feeling of being valued is created, and of contributing to a greater purpose. However, you will not find any favour in this book being accorded to 'discretionary effort', which essentially means getting people to do more work for no further reward. Why that ever became a 'thing' is a mystery to all but the beneficiaries.

The power of story within organizations cannot be underestimated, particularly where a transformation is being pursued. The author Steven James even refers to a story as "a transformation unveiled".[18] In an environment that embodies expression, it becomes possible for the members of an organization to originate and embed their own stories of positive experiences, underpinned by pride, loyalty and a genuine emotional connection. Their amalgamated effect helps to generate the values of the organization, or at least the organization *in that particular space*. These are not the values that the leadership team pick from a list of standard terms at an awayday at an overpriced hotel once every three or four years, but the real values held by all levels of the organization. To paraphrase Goethe,[19] stories are frozen culture.

Expression makes it possible to project these values to the outside world – not just to those visiting the space and carrying tales away with them – visibly underpinning an organization's commitment to social responsibility. This can extend into good works in the community, supporting local charitable or voluntary groups or initiatives, training people for related careers, or providing facilities for use by local groups. The expression of the organization through its space creates and strengthens this association, further generating pride and loyalty.

We should also remember that humanity is a brand and one that requires expression. We have the characteristics of a brand that is successful: we are clear about

---

18 Steven James, "The 5 Essential Story Ingredients," *WritersDigest.com*, May 9, 2014, http://www.writersdigest.com/online-editor/the-5-essential-story-ingredients.

19 Johann Peter Eckermann, *Gespräche mit Goethe in den letzten Jahren seines Lebens* ed. by Fritz Bergemann (Frankfurt am Main and Leipzig: Insel, 1987), p307.

– and continually communicate – who we are, what we stand for, what we offer, and why; we are authentic, and even when behind a mask we eventually reveal ourselves; we are carriers of emotion, are driven by emotion, and make an emotional connection with one another and the environment around us; we are of the same consistent genre, attracting loyalty and commitment – but each entirely unique, retaining an element of mystery and surprise; we are full of energy, passion and life; we stimulate all of the senses – sometimes we appeal to them; we create conversations; we have longevity, driven by evolution, adaptation and innovation; and our very existence changes others. In any environment, the overriding brand we see, feel and experience has to be human. We should start with the expression of humanity every time.

ENVIRONMENT

The importance of environment in workplace design, construction and operation is relatively recent, with accreditation schemes only beginning in the early 1990s. It now warrants its own category of consideration. Every workplace exists within an external environment and community, and should respond positively to it. There is nothing whatsoever to be lost by showing visible care and commitment to it. It is, in fact, a duty.

A fantastic workplace should be as environmentally responsible as possible, and the story deserves to be told. People generally want to work in and be associated with environmentally responsible organizations, a trend that has only been increasing in step with our awareness. Not only is such an approach hugely beneficial in itself, its reach and consequences are significant.

Care for the environment – as expressed through the workplace in terms of systems and services design, construction, use of materials, ethical sourcing, service and maintenance regimes, reduced carbon footprint, lower energy consumption, waste recycling programmes, elimination of the use of plastics, and the use of internal and external planting – is perceived to lie at the heart of an all-encompassing caring and ethically sound mindset that will inevitably extend to people – not just those who work for the organization, but those within its local community and the communities of all those affected by its operations and sourcing. It is hard to conceive of an organization that shows respect for the environment yet treats its people with disdain.

Procurement plays a significant role here. Procurement policies and decisions are vital in regard to environmental considerations, as they enable the filtering from use of harmful, unsustainable or ethically questionable materials, and of suppliers and service providers unable to provide sufficient evidence of sound environmental and ethical practices. A coherent and effective process can filter out negative influences at source.

Standards and accreditations are necessary visible illustrations of care, and we like to see the badges. Accreditation in this area is usually deemed important, but a compelling story can be as powerful and is a lot less expensive. Schemes such as BREEAM[20] (UK), LEED[21] (USA) and the newly published yet closely related WELL Standard[22] (developed in the USA; now being rolled out globally) rate the environmental and sustainable credentials of the design and construction of

20   BREEAM, accessed September 2, 2017, http://www.breeam.com/

21   LEED | USGBC, accessed September 2, 2017, https://new.usgbc.org/leed

22   International WELL Building Institute, accessed September 2, 2017, https://www.wellcertified.com/en

the building and workspace, as one-off assessments, while ratings such as the UK's Energy Performance Certificate (EPC)[23] evaluate performance in use. The EPC and its equivalents in other countries are becoming compulsory.

ETHER

If environment is a relatively new addition to the procession of 'e's, ether is newer still, and the most rapidly deepening of all six. Unlike environmental matters, however, which can be controlled and managed, this area can be much less so. It is possible only to influence it, with care.

In a world of instant accountability through social networking, creating a strong positive online association through the sharing of positive workplace experiences has become vital. This goes well beyond expression. Every organization exists physically and digitally, just as does every workplace. The digital space is one in which both positive and dangerous effects on the organization's brand and reputation can occur almost instantaneously. Our comparative inexperience in the digital space opens up the potential for both significant advantage and damage.

A fantastic workplace can make a huge contribution to the customer advocacy of an organization by creating a natural association with admirable values and looking after its people. Either through the voluntary sharing of positive views and stories on general social media or on specific sites in full swing at the time of writing (such as Glassdoor), the strength of the message lies in value. The voluntary element also underpins the role of the ether. While organizations seek to create advocacy themselves through their own social media teams, much of what is offered is freely given by those who have seen and experienced the workplace. Anonymity often ensures that the message is more strongly phrased and framed than would be otherwise. The robust and positive presence therefore of a fantastic workplace in digital space, in the ether, can support an organization's purpose, and draw potential customers and employees to it.

Of course, the workplace here is only a contributor. You may have the most effective, efficient, expressive and environmentally responsible workplace imaginable, but if people think the organization is deffective for other reasons entirely, it will be worth little or nothing. A great workplace alone will not save a rotten culture or reputation.

ENERGY

Wellbeing may have been an implicit factor in Duffy's original assessment of a workplace as efficient, but it is one of the key considerations of the age. Energy can be defined as "the strength and vitality required for sustained physical or mental activity".[24] The logic runs that fit, healthy and happy employees are more likely to be present (physically, emotionally, spiritually and intellectually), energized and productive. The idea of 'energy' provides a link between the physical workplace and its potential to support the wellbeing of its occupants.

The physical space you inhabit, whether at work, at home or socially, will be making a contribution either for or against your wellbeing. No space is neutral in this regard. It will either give you energy or sap it. You may deploy resilience if your space applies a negative influence, but this is no reason to ignore the positive contribution space is capable of making.

---

23   "Buying or Selling Your Home," gov.uk, accessed September 2, 2017,
        https://www.gov.uk/buy-sell-your-home/energy-performance-certificates

24   "Definition of Energy in English," Oxford Dictionaries, accessed September 2, 2017
        https://en.oxforddictionaries.com/definition/energy

Wellbeing in the broadest sense has become a subject of much focus since the beginning of this century, with a developing debate over whether organizations have a duty or even a responsibility to protect and enhance the wellbeing of their employees, given the time they spend working. Taking the workplace as an entity, it has the ability to make a specific contribution to individual wellbeing in two ways, outlined below. We will say more on this after a discussion of the Elements, when it will be clearer how the Elemental Workplace can operate as a wellbeing framework. The Elements collectively do not guarantee higher productivity, deeper innovation or greater quality of work, but they certainly make these things possible, and make for a better place to work.

Wellbeing is promoted through the architecture of the workplace, its interior design, mechanical and electrical systems, and installations. This all occurs without the conscious knowledge or participation of the occupants, unless they are particularly interested in the field. Secondly, it is promoted through the provision of amenities, facilities and services that enable better decision-making – on the part of all who use the space – concerning their own health and wellbeing.

In establishing this duality, the Elemental Workplace manages to avoid being drawn into a debate about personal responsibility and other influences on our wellbeing. The workplace should energize and vitalize the individual, and make a contribution to wellbeing. It should at any rate never create the conditions for the opposite.

PLAYING IT BACK

The six 'e's provide a rational framework for answering the vital question 'why?'. This can help generate the overriding vision for the workplace and is helpful at the Brief stage. Here are some examples of how our thinking around the six 'e's might be organized:

Efficiency	Can reduce overall space required by up to 30% Removes the need for – and cost of – churn Allows teams to grow, contract and flex Removes symbols of status and hierarchy Enables learning and development Enables beneficial change in ways of working
Effectiveness	Allows people to be at their best, every day Enables choice, promoting trust and transparency Enables people to work together – and alone Makes life simple, intuitive and easy Inspires, motivates and energizes Moves our thinking from 'my space' to 'our space'
Expression	Creates commitment through positive association Creates a feeling of being valued and appreciated Allows for origination of positive stories Creates a visible attraction and retention tool Fosters pride in the organization Supports social responsibility
Environment	Embeds safety and health at its heart Creates a commitment to the local community Visibly creates a culture of care Creates a more responsible supply chain Creates a visible commitment to sustainability Reduces carbon footprint and energy usage
Ether	Creates strong positive online association Encourages the sharing of positive stories Contributes to strong customer advocacy Creates a clear association with valuing people Creates a view of a 'great place to work' Supports the use of social tools for learning
Energy	Supports employee wellbeing Provides facilities to enable a healthy lifestyle Enables people to be fully present Supports a culture of care about people Increases the potential for performance Reduces absence and illness

In many respects, the typical starting Brief for most larger-scale workplace design projects often covers a number of common themes and ideas prompted by asking the question 'why?'. The age has generated some interchangeable and transferable ideas based on efficiency, effectiveness, environment and energy, interpreted through the lens of expression and externalized in the ether to create a unique proposition.

It would be surprising therefore if a modern Brief did not cover ideas developed from considering the six 'e's – such as flexibility, choice, visibility, mobility, serendipity, wellbeing, openness and transparency, togetherness and inclusion – irrespective of the type of organization, sector or location. The same terms revolve in the universal tombola. It is not a mere word game, however; through the Brief development process these ideas need to be continually understood and tested against the 'why?' One could usefully derive an Elemental Brief to guide the process.

Very often the 'why?' that appears in a framework such as the above is summarized in a few succinct sentences or phrases, or even a single phrase, as a project vision – for example, "to create a workplace that enables an energized, motivated and unified organization, with a clear sense of purpose and a desire to succeed". The structure becomes the first-line interpretation of that, and beyond will be second-, third- or even fourth-layer extrapolations of each.

So here, if needed, is the 'staircase pitch' (because we prefer not to use the elevator) distilling this chapter into a breathless between-floors justification for doing this:

Think what an amazing workplace could do for the business. We'll attract, keep and develop the most energized, motivated people, freely able to be their best, wanting to work in a place that reflects our dynamic, caring and responsible brand, proudly and openly sharing this enthusiasm, while we save up to a third of what we're spending on property that doesn't work for us to allow us to invest in an environment that does.

The importance here is not to lose sight of 'why?' this is being done, as that reasoning is unique and essential, and underpins the highest-level vision for the workplace. It can often be rubbed off the whiteboard never to be seen again. The 'why?' should be visible and consciously held through the entire journey and beyond. It should be repeated, ingrained and repeated again. It is the North Star of the project. In everything we are about to cover in this book, never lose sight of the 'why?'.

WHAT THIS BOOK WON'T TELL YOU

The Elemental Workplace will inform you of the components needed to create a fantastic workplace. However, it would be a mistake to assume that if you just follow these guidelines, it will all work out beautifully. It still requires a considerable degree of thought and application. There are no guides available that will give you all the answers. In managing your expectations, perhaps, it is worth identifying a few things that this book will not tell you. There are undoubtedly more, but these are the headlines.

WHAT YOUR SPACE SHOULD LOOK LIKE

We instinctively focus on what things will look like; we make the abstract real. We paint pictures in our head, and we collect references in this way. The design process often leaps the Brief stage, where it appears that nothing specific is happening, to get to where the fun begins: choosing the stuff that will surround you. The Elements featured here focus on functionality and contribution rather than aesthetics, types, styles or combinations.

There is no right or wrong 'look' for your organization. In the past two decades, we have moved away from the blended grey and beige – or what we might call 'greige' – that threw a cloak of inconsolable misery over most office environments, through snow-blinding minimalism, Google-generated play spaces and on to the 'workshop chic' of reclaimed furniture and the blinding discomfort of filament lightbulbs. The most recent trend has been to introduce more warmth through domestic influences, blurring the boundaries between our commonly inhabited spaces.

That is because it is all becoming just 'space'. We now perform a multitude of different tasks and functions in each space we occupy. We work at home, in hotels and on the high street; we play, dine and watch films in the office. Sectors that once preserved a distinct aesthetic that mirrored their function are now drawing in influences from other sectors; the borders are down. Never have the possibilities been greater, which presents a tremendous opportunity – and similarly, massive scope to goof it up (more on this later).

The Elements need to be in place, but you will still need to design the space. Far from making the design community unnecessary, the Elemental Workplace makes their role clearer and more important than ever.

WHAT WORKSTYLE WILL
BE BEST FOR YOU

The workplace as we know it today has been on a journey of its own since the earliest examples of what we call the 'modern office', such as the Time & Life building of the 1920s. This reflected the predominant management culture based on Frederick Taylor's 1911 study *The Principles of Scientific Management*,[25] where time and attendance are measured contributors to the view of effectiveness as optimization. From these rows of desks with close management supervision, we have seen the move to a 'landscape' (*Bürolandschaft*) approach in the 1950s and 1960s, to the introduction in the 1970s of cubicles in the form of systems furniture, to the social democratic offices of the 1980s, to the digital and then co-working spaces of the 2000s. It's not much of a history: no one has knowingly claimed the film rights.

During this evolution, spaces moved from open to almost entirely enclosed. Then, through the freedom that technology has brought us, we have returned to a more open style with more 'activity-based' and 'agile' workplaces that combine a shared approach with a range of work settings to support all forms of task. (In this book, a 'work setting' can be anywhere in a workplace where we stop to work, interact or socialize, whether it be a desk, meeting table, bench or something less formal – essentially a unit of the workplace.) In recent years journalists have been somewhat scathing of open environments, and as they hold the pen their voice has been heard. A sensational headline or two has helped.

Following *The Elemental Workplace* will not yield a strategic solution for the workplace type that best suits your organization now or the way you would like it to work – though it does include a strong advocacy of choice of space for particular work types. On this basis, it has an inherent leaning away from limited-range allocated space, but even in such an environment a degree of choice is still possible. A high-end law firm can still have an Elemental Workplace.

HOW TO MANAGE THE PROJECT

Though *The Elemental Workplace* is a guide to thought, planning, design and change, it does not detail how the team should be assembled or led, or what should be done

---

25 Frederick Winslow Taylor, *The Principles of Scientific Management* (repr. Scotts Valley, CA: CreateSpace Independent Publishing Platform, 2011).

at each stage. It can help keep the team focused on what is important, but there are no inbuilt mechanisms to ensure it happens – that is the role of the intelligent client, or the person leading the project on the client's behalf who has the relevant experience.

Whether the workplace project is a simple refresh or a full-scale relocation, a degree of professional help will probably be required. This usually amounts to a project manager, a cost consultant, workplace and engineering designers, and a safety consultant, with a series of sub-consultants as needed. If relocating, there will be property agents and lawyers involved as well. The importance of the intelligent client role cannot be overstated, as a professional team will do nothing without instruction, and will need to be directed and at times challenged. Invariably organizations are not resourced for such a spike in activity and expertise, and so the intelligent client role may need to be externally sourced and fully immersed in the organization's ways. It would be unfair to hand the role to an inexperienced but willing leader, and have them wait for the oncoming bus.

The organization will need its own governance and management structure too, to ensure that key decisions are taken or sanctioned (or both), and approved funds remain on tap. Very often this works best for a larger organization as a two-tier structure: an executive or advisory board that enables the most senior leadership to be involved in the project (or at least visibly associated with its aims), supported by a more active 'exec-minus-one'-level steering group.

There are no right or wrong ways to organize, but these suggestions are tried and tested, and can serve as a useful starting point.

HOW TO PLAN CHANGE

We touched in the opening chapter on the reality that this will be a change project, of which creating the workplace will be a part. Project managers like to see the programme in linear form, holding as they do a firm but misplaced belief in Newtonian time. Yet it rarely occurs that way – it is iterative, chaotic and messy. They,along with the rest of the participants in the journey, will need to understand this fundamental principle, as it will alter the normal dynamic.

A little more is offered later on how to think about the change journey, but for now the key message is that the project started before you thought it did, and will continue beyond where you think it will end. All work-space exists in a state of permanent 'beta trial' (an idea being live-tested with consumers). Workspace itself is a journey, not a product. As Robert Propst said in his work *The Office: A Facility Based on Change*: "We must be allowed to change our minds. We must be allowed to respond to errors as they emerge."[26] We are not attempting to create a perfection that we can stand back and admire. To refer to *Parkinson's Law* once again, "Perfection, we know, is finality; and finality is death."[27]

It is at this point that we need to reflect on the thinking of the original (arguably the best, and possibly even the only) change consultant, Heraclitus, writing in Ephesus in the mid-6th century BCE. His doctrine of flux has been

---

26   Robert Propst, *The Office: A Facility Based on Change* (Elmhurst, IL: The Business Press, 1968).

27   C. Northcote Parkinson, *Parkinson's Law* (Houghton Mifflin, 1957), p61.

paraphrased (as he didn't leave us any written work of his own, and we are therefore reliant on the writing of Diogenes) innumerable times, but it still needs restating. The most famous and succinct phrase attributed to him is "All is flux" – everything moves, nothing remains still. It creates an absurdity of the oft-found utterance on any project that "people do not like change", as people *are* change. It is the human essence.

HOW YOUR CULTURE WILL BE IMPACTED

The phrase "Culture eats design for breakfast" is often heard in workplace circles, paraphrasing a regularly uttered statement about strategy attributed, rightly or wrongly, to Peter Drucker. Rarely does anyone know what it means; it just sounds lofty and complicates where it need not, by assuming that intangible notions will conspire against us. Most struggle to describe what culture means, too, and rarely are one definition and another alike; it's the stuff of conversations after the bar has closed.

Very often, workplace transformation is seen as an investment that will help fix cultural problems. A new workplace will certainly influence local culture, yet the nature, degree and likelihood of positive impact are almost impossible to assess, being bound up with other internal and external influences in play at the time. To pin all hopes on workplace alone is unfair – it has to be partnered with an awareness of the issues and a willingness to change behaviours and processes from the top down. It is again a matter of balance: physical workplace in tandem with visible senior-level commitment. Behaviour is often modelled to a far greater extent than instructions are followed.

Most problems of – and therefore solutions to – organizational culture usually reside in management and leadership. Physical workplace changes supportive of resolving them are the taking down of physical barriers (walls, offices), increased visibility of leadership and a conscious reduction in management-by-presence. Conversely, poorly designed and with inappropriate or inadequate change enablement, these actions may exacerbate the issues. Culture may well eat design for breakfast, if we let it. Let's not let it. Better that they have breakfast together.

It is also of note that the idea of 'culture' is fragmented, localized and disparate. Rarely does a whole organization occupy a single space, yet it is often rolled up into the generalization that every space in every location reflects the same organizational culture. It does not, of course: there are often microcultures within large spaces. Cultures vary within and between locations. Unless an organization resides in a single space, the cultural impact will be felt in that location only, with the *potential* to ripple outwards if the changes it drives are significant enough and there are means for stories to carry. A transformed workplace with demonstrable leadership commitment has significant potential to contribute to positive cultural change, but it still needs to be delivered effectively – and elementally.

WHAT THE FUTURE LOOKS LIKE

Contemplation of the future of work is rife, stemming essentially from fascination with how technology will shape us, how we relate to one another, what we do and how we do it. A day barely goes by without an established commentator pondering the future of work and what the future workplace will look like. We project our imagination with all the accuracy of the Martians in the 1960s Cadbury's Smash (instant mashed potato) advertisements, laughing uncontrollably as they watch humans peeling potatoes. We have had Workplace 2020, Workplace 2030, Workplace 2050. We have literally thousands of amateur trend-spotters taking pot-shots at the wind. There is no harm in doing so: it's fun, as long as it is not positioned as anything other than fun.

The Elemental Workplace is applicable to the workplace of today – the present that so few are reluctant to talk about – and tomorrow – the future we have very little idea about. That is because it applies universally to all office environments. The changes likely to take place in the coming years will still be against the backdrop of office environments. The impact of AI, space-as-a-service, the 'gig economy' and the unbridled pessimism of VUCA (volatile, uncertain, complex and ambiguous – a term originating in military use in the 1990s to describe the modern world) as a world view are among many topics that consume energy and emotion but have no bearing on the Elemental Workplace. Its interpretation may change, as may its physical appearance and the technology deployed, but, at the end of the day, if people are working in a space with other people, it will remain relevant.

The groundwork complete, hopefully you would like to carry on reading.

PART TWO

HOW
(FIRST FIX)

HOW: WORKPLACE DESIGN PRINCIPLES

This chapter considers our mindset in approaching a workplace transformation. While focusing on the 12 Elements is vital in creating a fantastic workplace, a number of principles apply to the design process itself. As the Elements are independent of the desired outcome, so too are these principles, whether you are an internet start-up or a stalwart department store furnishing your dreams in walnut. As it is a matter of the blend, they are in no particular order. Each of the design principles described below can be applied to each of the Elements.

BE SMART-ISH

Gather evidence – but *only just enough* (in this I am paraphrasing a statement made in conversation by Lloyd Davis, the founder of the Tuttle Club and a very early social networker) – and thereafter focus on opportunities to allow people to choose to do things differently. The view of the future workplace should comprise a balance between evidence of what occurs at present, and opportunities for the future. Evidence should be both quantitative and qualitative, statistical data and story. There is as much insight and power in small stories as there is in heaps of statistical data – in their own way, stories *are* data. Creating a fantastic workplace is an open-ended road trip. The rear-view mirror, your evidence, is for safety. What is ahead is far more intriguing.

BE BETA

As mentioned in Part One, we need to bear in mind that space itself is a journey not a product, a permanent beta trial, which means you are also enabling change long after the space is 'finished'. Heraclitus would have approved of this approach. Too many change programmes wind down a few weeks after the last move. Very often the success of one space or area militates against the success of another, and invariably this occurs over time as people get to understand the space. It is important to continually observe, test, discuss, measure and be prepared to tweak and change the space, because no one wants to wait 15 years for the next crusade. It is also worth remembering that an agile workplace takes much more of this form of managing than a static 1:1 arrangement. However, whatever view we take of the space, changes in the organization through organic growth, contraction, or mergers and acquisitions could dictate what happens next. The organization rarely stands still, so the space will need to move with it.

BRIEF, NOT BRIEF

Time must be spent on the Brief. It may sound obvious, but you have to write it down. It is the most important work you will undertake on any workplace creation. A great deal of the time you will be talking to yourself, to ensure it is what you want. There is nothing wrong with a bit of self-doubt, but it is best to get it out of the way before you start the project. It is important during this process that we talk to people like adults, listen carefully and understand but be prepared to challenge: we should not be waiters taking orders. The Brief will refer to both the Elements and the ephemera, as it is outcome-focused in a manner that the Elements are not. It is also worth remembering that the Brief is not the solution – it is an aspiration drawn from the data and stories captured and the possibilities the journey prompts. If the Brief looks like a design, it *is* a design and you have not created a Brief. Go back.

BE CLEAR

We seem to exist in an age where there is an almost institutional pressure to be 'disruptive' and create stunted output-specification Briefs that make us feel 'uncomfortable'. While they are entertaining to hear about, they are not especially helpful. We should avoid trying to be too clever with people's productivity, wellbeing and comfort in the name of corporate vanity, as nine times out of ten it will bite you on the very same smart arse deployed in conceiving of the Brief (that is, the nine times we never hear about – more on this towards the end of the book).

BALANCE LIKE A BALLERINA

As we stated in the section on "Ridiculous myths", the workplace 'industry' continually lurches from one major idea (or panacea) to the other, awaiting the epoch-defining idea that stubbornly refuses to arrive. It will not, ever. We always rock back on the pendulum to the balance point, when the latest fad proves to be just that and peters out in a little embarrassment and denial. As the Gensler *Workplace Survey*[28] points out every few years, we generally spend around half of our time working alone and half working with others. That is a good enough starting point for just about every workplace scheme. Wherever there appears to be a leaning too far in a particular direction, pull it back.

---

28   *2013 US Workplace Survey* (Gensler, 2013).

HUMAN BEING FIRST, AESTHETIC SECOND

The installations have to work. If you can get them looking beautiful too, that is delightful – beauty always has a place in any scheme. Yet very often aesthetics and ergonomics have to step outside to settle the matter. Ergonomics should always win. We want beautiful things, but beautiful things that work. More energy still needs to be channelled into beautifying ergonomic solutions.

INCLUDE

This is both a design principle – a reference point for all the Elements – and an Element in its own right. By definition, just about every installation and space excludes to some extent. Steve Maslin of Building User Design[29] is an excellent resource in this area of practice. But, suffice to say, as many people as possible must be able to experience and enjoy as much of every workspace as possible. As mentioned above, most of the time we find the beauty of the form militating against inclusion and it is a constant struggle to remain inclusive while delivering a space that is aesthetically appealing. Inclusion, like ergonomics, should always win.

SIMPLIFY

Simple is not simplistic. Workplace is not a complicated subject, despite the attempts of many to make it so (and hence this book). Do not overcomplicate the Brief, the typologies, the segmentation. There is no better quote than Antoine de Saint-Exupéry's "Perfection is achieved not when there is nothing left to add, but when there is nothing left to take away."[30] If you are starting to lose the thread or not understand it, imagine how your colleagues will feel.

STAY RELEVANT

Fads can be expensive when they are woven through the workplace. You are quite probably not Google, and are unlikely to be Google, but by all means learn how and why they do what they do with their space and then decide if there is anything in it for you. Consider the approach, methodology, thought process, and permissions, but not the outcome. Give your design a lifeline beyond the initial dopamine rush. The contribution of Google's famous slide has been vital – we now think differently, more expansively. As a point of relevance, however, it has passed.

SWEAT THE SMALL STUFF

The success of the workplace scheme is so very often rooted in the most practical and personal detail. Once it is established, spend less time on repeatedly chiseling the mission statement and more on what it means to people at the micro level. At a stage sooner than you anticipate, they will look through your grand ambitions to see if their locker is big enough for their shoes and whether there is space in the kitchen for their muesli. As buildings should be designed from the inside out (but rarely are), so workplace should be designed from the kitchen cupboard out. Contrary to popular phraseology, it *is* possible to think of everything, and because you care you have to think of everything. Start making a list.

---

29 Building User Design Solutions Ltd., accessed September 12, 2017, http://www.buildinguserdesignsolutions.co.uk/

30 Antoine de Saint-Exupéry, *Terres des Hommes* (Paris: Gallimard, 1963) p47.

SCOPE: THE SOCIAL WORKPLACE

SPACE, PHYSICAL AND DIGITAL

In the social workplace, we are fundamentally connected to our colleagues, and we work as one with them. We still need all the aspects of the physical workplace that are deemed Elemental, but in thinking and responding to them we need an increasing awareness of the digital sphere in which we live and work, the increasingly social nature of our working environment, and how we use the physical environment to enable and support our participation in digital space.

Consider this interpretation. We would likely see the individual buried away in a quiet corner, headphones on, intensely staring into a laptop as performing solo, focused work, possibly writing a report or creating a project plan. Meanwhile we see the huddle of people around a high table on the fringe of the café strewn with papers and gadgets as collaborating, possibly catching up on the progress of a project or planning a new one. Yet the solo worker in our example may be interacting in real time with thousands of people around the world, sharing knowledge and connecting people. The group in the café may be talking about yesterday's television. Appearances of activity will become increasingly deceptive. A deeper awareness and understanding is vital.

The Elemental Workplace is all about physical space. The workplace, however, no longer ends there. Our scope, and our opportunity for insight, extends to the digital workplace too. Before this century began, we would have considered the 'social' workplace to be a chat at the rusty tea urn and extended Friday lunchtime drinks. External to interactions within the organization, professional bodies brought like-minded souls together. Knowledge was captured and stored in physical form, and roller-racking and "the misery of manila folders" (from Roethke's poem, quoted in the opening chapter) were rife. Much has changed. Technology has not made us more sociable, but it has enabled us to explore our innate sociability more freely, openly and regularly.

Interestingly, 'social' interaction is still too often seen and understood as personal, non-productive activity that takes place during a break from 'work'. To even the more enlightened, the forms of social interaction that take place using tools in the public domain are often deemed trivial. Yet we increasingly exist in both the physical and digital spheres, and the latter will only increase. The digital sphere is intrinsically social, shared by all. Within large organizations often spread across continents, using a combination of email, open drives and internet portals, the problems of sharing knowledge, locating critical expertise, and co-creation and co-innovation are too intangible for traditional functions to contemplate. This collection of activities is often called 'social capital'. For many organizations, at the time of writing an awareness of the power of social capital is in its infancy. *The Social Organization* by Jon Ingham[31] is worth reading for a deeper understanding.

Yet, the more our existence and participation within the digital sphere grows, and organizations begin to understand this and respond, the more that physical space will become part of a broader idea of simply 'space', the tangible and intangible as one. How we perceive activity will change too. When we consider digital space in the same manner as thinking about physical space, we mean the tools (external networks and platforms, and internal enterprise social networks) and the associated behaviours and practices that they enable. We therefore need a broader consideration of the workplace. Effectively, physical space + digital space = social workplace.

There may have been an articulation of this meshing before the idea of digital space was even conceived, in the philosophy of Kitaro Nishida (1870-1945).[32] He proposed the concept of *ba*, a shared space for the development of emerging relationships that may be physical or mental, or any combination of them. Development of the idea by others[33] has included digital space, and it has become a key principle in the field of knowledge management. It is perhaps a little puzzling that the workplace community has not embraced the idea more fully, but this may reflect a tendency of the idea towards the abstract. It also perhaps indicates that at the time of writing the workplace community is struggling to grasp the relationship between physical and digital space, attempting more to pull down ideas from the digital into the physical and replicate them rather than embracing their fundamentally inseparable nature.

Yet for all the time and attention devoted to creating opportunities for chance encounters in physical space, as covered in our earlier consideration of effectiveness, there exists a massive potential for this to happen in the digital sphere. Social networks such as Facebook, Twitter and Instagram, and those enterprise social networks within the organization's firewall, all enable easy search for like-minded souls with similar interests and the chance of discovering people and activities that would have been

31 Jon Ingham, *The Social Organization* (London: Kogan Page, 2017).

32 Kitaro Nishida, *An Inquiry into the Good*, trans. M Abe and C Ives (New Haven: Yale University Press, 1990).

33 Ikujiro Nonaka and Noboru Konno, "The Concept of Ba': Building Foundation for Knowledge Creation," *California Management Review*, Vol. 40, No. 3 (Spring 1998), p40-54.

almost impossible when confined to a physical space. A post by John Stepper[34] identifies the closeness we can often feel when developing online relationships through active use of these platforms for work as "kinship", and refers to an earlier article by Clive Thompson in the *New York Times*[35] that draws attention to the "ambient awareness" that can be created in the digital sphere, offering a similar experience to that we obtain from face-to-face social interaction. This is the social workplace in action.

FROM MILTON KEYNES TO SOHO

We are back to efficiency and effectiveness again for a moment, to consider how different approaches to physical space can influence social behaviour in the workplace.

The understanding of the workplace pursued in this book is that of an inhabited space. Much has been written in recent years about the workplace being 'all about people' and 'human-centric'. It is difficult to imagine an environment being created for habitation that is *not* focused on people, but much of this stems from the commercial pressure of *efficiency* trumping the human-oriented need for *effectiveness*. This was covered in the chapter "Why create a fantastic workplace?" but merits a brief mention in regard to the social workplace. The effectiveness of the workplace drives its social capabilities, and creates the possibility of social interaction.

Efficiency of space starts with the property developer needing to maximize the size of the building on the plot of land, through to creating the maximum amount of rentable space possible and letting it for the longest period of time that the market will sustain to the person most able to pay the bill.

It is a mission driven by efficiency. The outcome from a plot of available land, a willing developer, a malleable local authority planning department and a suitcase full of cash can be over-occupied, characterless vanilla boxes that the occupiers detest. At the time of writing this is at last being challenged.

The most consistently restrictive feature of workplace design in the decade of social enlightenment has been the straight line. In terms of urban metaphor, this can be characterized as people wanting an unstructured, unpredictable and surprising space, such as London's Soho with its twists and nooks, but being gifted the rigidity and ruled lines of 1960s new town Milton Keynes. That may be harsh on the Buckinghamshire settlement, but in workplace terms Milton Keynes is easier and cheaper to plan, build, occupy, maintain and flex. In Taylorist terms it is 'optimized', created in the one and only best way. In addition, its openness and regularity are in keeping with the trend of the late 1990s and early 2000s towards the 'open plan' style so derided by … well, most people. Milton Keynes also represents a symbol of control. Its openness and predictability support an approach to management that we shall look at in the later section on "Choice".

The effectiveness of Soho could also be debated, but is derived from its social enablement. It creates the possibility of multiple levels of human interaction, or, equally importantly, human isolation. It creates places to be seen,

---

34 John Stepper, "The Best Office Design for Collaboration is also the Cheapest", *LinkedIn*, July 12, 2016, https://www.linkedin.com/pulse/best-office-design-collaboration-also-cheapest-john-stepper

35 Clive Thompson, "Brave New World of Digital Intimacy", *New York Times*, September 5, 2008, http://www.nytimes.com/2008/09/07/magazine/07awareness-t.html?pagewanted=all&_r=0

and to hide. Its constantly churning population and the regenerating youth of its establishment create continual surprise and interest. Control in such a space is seen as elusive; it symbolizes a healthy degree of freedom and self-orientation. Its less desirable aspects are disregarded in favour of what it contributes, to the individual and to groups. In many ways, it represents the unpredictability and opportunity of digital space. Robert Propst, considering in the late 1960s the similarity of office and city planning, described this struggle as "humanity versus geometry".[36] The social workplace, to be effective and productive, needs a deliberate injection of *inefficiency*.

The social workplace therefore further underlines the care needed in the balance between efficiency and effectiveness.

DIGITAL CONTEXT

There are a number of interesting contrasts between the physical and digital workplaces that may help this understanding grow. I am indebted to the work and thinking of Luis Suárez (at www.elsua.net), which prompted the development of this section. It is often the case that ideas from the digital sphere are simply drawn down for use within the physical, with an expectation that their use will be identical. Contrasting their respective use will give us a much greater insight as we progress through the Elements and consider how to enable change, so it is worth taking a few moments to consider.

First, **communities** and **neighbourhoods** are words often used interchangeably within the workplace sector, yet they mean different things. The former are consciously free of physical boundaries and even go as far as to deny them;

the latter are defined by them. We are looking for them to achieve the same thing – connection, sharing, collective development, and generally being good or even excellent to each other (what we might call the 'Bill & Ted' approach, from the 1989 film *Bill & Ted's Excellent Adventure*, which might just be the only HR policy you will ever need). As the digital sphere is free of physical boundaries, the idea of communities is more readily in use, while in the physical domain we focus more on the notion of neighbourhoods. An effective workplace change approach should be based on the idea of being a good neighbour and acting in a neighbourly manner – which we instinctively recognize without needing a slide deck to explain it – while adopting a community spirit to encourage sharing within and beyond physical boundaries. In this way, we achieve the best of both.

Talk of community often leads to a discussion of 'Dunbar's Number'.[37] Although the British anthropologist didn't actually spell out the number 150, it has been taken as an approximation from his work in the early 1990s as the maximum effective community size – the number of people we can know and relate to – given the size of the human brain. It has been a feature of workplace design ever since, with some organizations using it as a guide to the maximum number of people permitted in a single space. There are no hard and fast rules around this, but practice tends to indicate that 100-150 is a manageable number within a defined area such as a floor or discrete part-floor, from which we derive neighbourhood size. Actual community sizes

---

36 Robert Propst, *The Office: A Facility Based on Change* (Elmhurst, IL: The Business Press, 1968).

37 R. I. M. Dunbar, "Neocortex Size as a Constraint on Group Size in Primates," *Journal of Human Evolution*, Vol. 22 No. 6, (1992) p469–493.

will be self-regulated by each individual as these will comprise a subset of colleagues within the physical area, in addition to those people known in the digital sphere.

Interestingly, the idea of community has been embraced by the co-working movement, to capture a sense of equal and binding contribution to the social life of a space occupied by independent and otherwise unrelated groups. This is a harnessing of the community spirit that still seeks neighbourly behaviour.

Secondly, consider the difference between **adoption** and **adaptation**. Adoption is an unhelpful way to look at how we change behaviour. As a plan-driven, predictive methodology, it comes with a shoehorn – it implies compliance. Workplace professionals are always talking about people 'adopting' new behaviours in a new space. However, this approach negatively impacts change and requires a huge effort to overcome its connotations. Adaptation, as a value-driven methodology, is far more effective and powerful. Hence, we have the idea of 'early adapters'. Adaptation respects the individual's experiential journey and allows each person the time they need, allowing the individual to come to their own conclusion about the benefit of the change, which as a result becomes deeply embedded. The process is not always slow; it can be quicker than an adoptive approach and will likely require less tension and less reworking. Adoption, by contrast, is often fragile and superficial, giving only the illusion of success.

Thirdly, there are contrasts between the groups we engage as **change agents**. The digital world seeks out more junior participants (irrespective of age) – those who are less likely to make do, who have the time to help others and to whom a questioning attitude comes naturally. The process relies on intuition and experimentation rather than training;

it is about enabling change through the delight of discovery. In workplace change programmes, on the other hand, we naturally look to more senior individuals to lead change – those with access to resources, obligatory shoehorns and the ability to 'unblock' (i.e. force). They are focused on addressing the resistors, as opposed to the digital workplace's strategy of harnessing the enlightened. There is much of Peter Fryer's 'Trojan mice'[38] idea about the digital workplace that the physical workplace must learn from: the releasing of many small ideas on the basis that some may take hold and create significant change – along, of course, with a little patience; a workplace scheme needs both.

Fourthly, we come to the difference between **education** (push) and **enablement** (pull). The online world looks to model and demonstrate behaviour to enable a change of behaviour in others. In the world of workplace there is a deeply unfortunate tendency to instruct and inform, the dreaded 'etiquette training' that is woven into so many change programmes, in a bid to *drive* adoption. Everyone does it, so everyone continues to do it. The digital world seems much more comfortable with people changing at varying speeds – adapting – given that generally the tools come first and the usage thereafter, allowing existing behaviour to be phased out. Both old and new worlds invariably exist alongside one another. In the physical world, there is the limitation that when the new space is ready, the old space is entirely left behind and we invariably drop everyone in at once, expecting that they will apply what they have been told beforehand. We must still respect

---

38   Trojan Mice, accessed September 12, 2017, www.trojanmice.com

individual journeys – and once people know that we will, their perspective will change too. Those we often see as resistors will just be those on a different journey; we lose the classification entirely.

Fifth is the difference in the uses of **progress measurement**. In the digital workplace we measure progress but rarely publish it, to avoid focusing on the metric instead of the transformation process. It can take a year to 18 months for behaviours to bed in, before we can tell positive stories. In the physical world there is a far greater expectation of immediate results that we broadcast to all, driven by the pressure to report ROI. Everyone is desperate to know that the change has 'worked'. This approach stifles the individual journey and underpins the obsession with adoption. The digital workplace seems much more comfortable with being able to describe the negative ROI of *not doing anything at all* (an idea for which I owe credit to Ellen Trude, in conversation). Again, so much more patience would be beneficial.

Sixth is the place in each sphere of **efficiency**. While Taylorist commercial sensibilities tend towards the goal of optimization of people, process and resources within the 'One Best Way', the digital workplace thrives on inefficiency to be effective. The notion of serendipity so often quoted in the modern-day workplace design Brief took hold most notably in digital space, where social tools allowed the pursuit of tangents and promoted accidental discoveries and encounters. The notion of 'stumbling on' people and ideas in digital space is fundamental to their spread and benefit, even though there can be drawbacks too, such as where self-reinforcing 'bubbles' can lead to a distorted view of the world. Physical space has tried to mirror this, creating collision points – "you *will* bump into each other, damn it!". The essence of digital space, however, is that no such forcing is necessary; the activities of the participants create this serendipity, underpinned by acceptance of the 'gift economy' (where things of value are not traded but are freely exchanged without any expectation of reward) and a mutually supportive culture. In this, the physical workplace is playing catch-up. The backlash in some quarters against an often-simplistic view of open space suggests that the struggle may be more prolonged than it seemed at first thought.

Lastly, there is a contrast in **making things happen** between the plan/deliver approach of the physical workplace and the do-something-today approach of the digital. In a reversal of the application of patience, so often needed in the physical domain, the digital workplace is this time the fidgety one where even the smallest signs of progress can be important. This underpins the Agile Engineering approach to software development. Poor-quality environments do not need to await the wholesale mobilization of the project – small changes can always benefit. As we have stated already, every physical workplace is in permanent beta, so even those coming to the end of their useful lives can be improved.

A restless spirit and a willingness to get things done, a belief that things can be done rather than a list of reasons why they cannot, and a clear sense that we are all in it together – that has got to be a worthwhile adaptation from the digital to the physical which we can take with us into a discussion of each of the Elements.

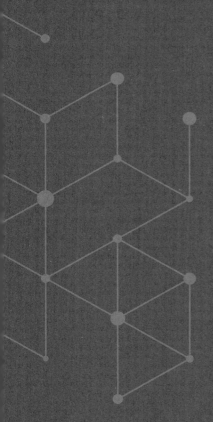

PART THREE

WHAT

THE 12
WORKPLACE
ELEMENTS

We have considered why we need a fantastic workplace, reflected on how the physical workplace is merging with the digital and its implications for our thinking about physical space and change, and reviewed a simple set of design principles that have helped us adopt a practical mindset.

The next 12 sections of the book deal in turn with each of the Elements. They are as follows, and are discussed in no specific order, as they are each considered as important as the others:

1 **Da** Daylight				2 **Co** Connectivity
3 **Sp** Space	4 **Ch** Choice	5 **In** Influence	6 **Cn** Control	7 **Re** Refresh
8 **Se** Sense	9 **Cf** Comfort	10 **Ic** Inclusion	11 **Wa** Wash	12 **St** Storage

While each Element is intended to be as stand-alone and portable as possible, there are relationships between them, mostly positive but occasionally needing caution. It is recommended that the Elements be considered together as a whole, and that cross-references are taken account of.

You will likely think of more Elements as you progress, which is expected and encouraged. If you believe you have uncovered something worthy of inclusion, please drop a line to the email address given in the opening chapter. This is, after all, an ever-evolving body of work, a permanent beta of its own. My thanks to you for considering how the proposition may be improved for the benefit of those who occupy your workspace.

DAYLIGHT

1 **Da** Daylight				**2** **Co** Connectivity
3 **Sp** Space	**4** **Ch** Choice	**5** **In** Influence	**6** **Cn** Control	**7** **Re** Refresh
8 **Se** Sense	**9** **Cf** Comfort	**10** **Ic** Inclusion	**11** **Wa** Wash	**12** **St** Storage

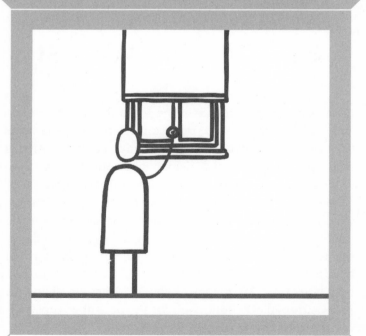

As with several of the Workplace Elements, the need for daylight extends into the deepest mists of time. We have known about, forgotten and rediscovered the need for daylight. It generally comes top in any 'live' straw poll on which Workplace Element is most important to us, as we instinctively reach for it wherever possible. There is a sense that if we are bathed in natural light, we can deal with everything else.

Daylight regulates our lives and everything that supports our lives. With the rotation of the earth it orders our circadian system, or 'body clock' as we often call it, and that of just about every living organism. It is interesting that in a world where routine and repetition are increasingly challenged and disparaged, the importance of the circadian system is becoming recognized, as if an underlying stability is needed for us to be able to then express ourselves. This is particularly so where it relates to the digital intrusion into our sleep – that is, our inability to leave our smartphones alone for seven to eight hours a night, even when legislation tells us to.

What we do know is that daylight is nature's antiseptic. Florence Nightingale in her *Notes on Nursing* (first published in 1860) identified speedier recovery times in patients who had access to daylight, observing that "a dark house is always an unhealthy house",[39] a view supported by numerous credible research studies since. It assists with the treatment of depression and helps combat levels of stress that give rise to obesity and heart conditions. At the core of our being we deeply and intuitively understand that we need it. Lock yourself in a basement conference room all day listening to talks about wellbeing, and you crave the light. On surfacing, your eyes smart as it pierces your retinas, but the sense of relief is palpable.

---

39   Florence Nightingale, *Notes on Nursing* (New York: D Appleton & Company, 1860), p28.

There is also a great deal of misinformation regarding daylight and the workplace, due to the over-generalization of what it means to have natural light in an office environment. The direction of light, distance from windows, as well as the use and control of shading systems all confuse the picture. When publications such as the *Human Spaces* report[40] claim that 42% of European office employees have no natural light in their working environment, we are instinctively shocked but do not really know what that means. We just know that this is not right and that something should be done to redress it. We also have to show caution when making claims of a correlation between daylight and productivity; as we have seen, we have yet to understand exactly what the latter means and to separate its subjective and objective perspectives.

We should not immediately decry the use of artificial light. The invention in 1926 by Edmund Germer of the fluorescent tube enabled far greater areas of internal space to be utilized by creating up to five times as much light, flicker-free and with excellent colour definition. We still need the best-quality, well maintained and clean artificial installations to provide lighting during seasonal changes, and to balance the fluctuations in natural light from the weather. Daylight is not a constant resource; its availability varies widely across the planet and through the seasons.

It is also the case that daylight is often confused with the idea of views or vistas. We cannot have the external view without the equal and opposite penetration of daylight (window film permitting). The research findings in the *Human Spaces* report[41] list a view of the sea as the fourth most desirable characteristic of an office. However, in central business districts it is just as likely that the source of daylight also creates a vista onto a crisp-packet-strewn courtyard and a host of air-conditioning fan units.

The essential Element is daylight; the views are entirely dependent upon location. What we need to do with views, however, is not squander them – if there is a view of the sea (unlikely as this is through an office window), as many as possible should be able to enjoy it. There is considerable debate as to whether views can be inspiring or distracting, and so focusing social and communal space around views requires much consideration.

What we need to see as an Elemental construct is access to as much daylight in the workplace as possible, to provide a permanent visual connection to the external environment. Some countries have legislated to this effect, reflecting the importance attached to it. There is no 'ideal' working position in relation to daylight that might be feasible for everyone; indeed, when we look at the Element of Choice, we make it possible for people to take the time they need closer to daylight, and select other, deeper-set areas for other tasks as needed.

We also have to bear in mind within the Element of Inclusion that there are light-sensitive conditions that require a particular response that works against exposure to as much daylight as possible. There may also be tasks, such as detailed film and graphics editing, that require very low levels of ambient light to ensure the required focus on detail. Daylight should be plentiful and readily available, but not universally compulsory.

We need to do everything possible to let the daylight in; what we then choose to do with it is up to us.

------

40 "Human Spaces: The Global Impact of Biophilic Design in the Workplace", *Interface*, 2015, http://humanspaces.com/global-report/

41 Ibid.

CONNECTIVITY

1 **Da** Daylight				**2** **Co** Connectivity
3 **Sp** Space	**4** **Ch** Choice	**5** **In** Influence	**6** **Cn** Control	**7** **Re** Refresh
8 **Se** Sense	**9** **Cf** Comfort	**10** **Ic** Inclusion	**11** **Wa** Wash	**12** **St** Storage

Fix the technology. Fix it now. In many respects, it has nothing whatsoever to do with a workplace project. Even if there is no workplace project, fix it. In an age when every organization is an information technology organization, and just about everyone uses some form of computer and has a degree of IT-literacy, not providing high-speed, reliable connectivity for employees and visitors (hassle-free, for both) and the most powerful, lightest and portable computer is entirely counter-productive. As we have established, somewhere around 85% of an organization's non-core costs are its people and only 5% the IT, so to leave them toothless is without excuse. We would not hire lumberjacks, give them a blunt saw and expect them to cut down trees.

Connectivity unleashes potential; it enables connectedness, an aim of both the physical and digital workplace. Without efficient and effective connectivity, the doorway to the wonders and opportunities of the digital workplace is rusty-bolted. The digital workplace will grow in importance relative to the physical in the coming decades, and therefore the need for the best possible connectivity will grow with it. Without the digital workplace there is no genuinely social workplace.

We can operate effectively in short bursts in a poor workplace with excellent IT and connectivity – as we do in less than ergonomic, noisy and insecure public spaces such as cafés – yet not the other way around. Despite the clamour in almost every organization, you should not have to 'bring your own device' (BYOD) to make up for the shortcomings of what is provided. BYOD should be a scheme to create choice, not a cheeky residual fix.

Part of the difficulty in many organizations relates to the method of budgeting and its respective procurement challenges. When systems are built bottom up, downward pressure on computer equipment costs results in essential components and functionality being stripped out in order to achieve the minimum possible standards, rather than looking at what it is possible to provide, and the functionality it may bring. An organization deciding to run laptop replacement on a four-year cycle instead of three (when perhaps two might be more suitable), and to remove SSD cards from laptops to save a small amount per device, has not considered the disproportionately negative impact that this tiny saving will have on workplace mobility. While the cost per person is minuscule compared to even a moderate workplace fit-out, it is often not included within the workplace transformation budget. It should be, and it should be the first, inviolable line.

It's not all about wifi; not at the time of writing, anyway. We have had wifi commercially since 1999, and it is now almost ubiquitous in commercial buildings, with varying degrees of signal strength, coverage and bandwidth. Wifi signal strength can be affected by the structure of the building, particularly when metal and water are involved. Even a flowerpot can cause interruption. The standards we expect while working in the urban environment and at home are very different from those we expect in an office. Cat-6 (or whatever will be next) will still be required in an office environment for use when stationed, now that USB docking stations for instant plug-and-play that support most forms of laptop hardware are ubiquitous and affordable. That leaves wifi capacity available for those who are roaming or working in short-stay or informal settings.

There is also the matter of telephony. Voice over Internet Protocol (VoIP) has virtually replaced the traditional private branch exchange (PBX) telephone system within most organizations and it is now commonplace for voice calls to be routed through the personal computer and handled using a headset instead of a desktop handset, allowing the service to be available wherever there is an internet connection. In many cases the ubiquity of the mobile phone in all its guises has reduced the dependence upon any form of corporate telephony for purely voice calls. Much of the available bandwidth in a corporate network, however, is often taken up by the sharing of content on VoIP calls, so, despite the use of the mobile phone, there is still a demand for highly effective connectivity for calls combining voice and data.

Having provided excellent connectivity, a plug-and-play environment (even where desks are assigned) and above-requirements kit, everything has to work. All of the time. It needs to be simple and easy to obtain help, and to service additional or particular needs. A 'genius lounge' or service desk staffed by knowledgeable people with a commitment to service is not difficult to provide even in smaller workplaces. Keeping the technology fixed is as important as fixing it now.

It may sound counter-intuitive, but connectivity sets people free like nothing else. While the power of the 10% of total organizational costs – the workplace – to unleash the potential of its people is enormous, without technology's 5% contribution its impact in the modern world is limited. They are inseparable. Fix the technology. Fix it now.

SPACE

1 Da Daylight				**2 Co** Connectivity
3 Sp Space	**4 Ch** Choice	**5 In** Influence	**6 Cn** Control	**7 Re** Refresh
8 Se Sense	**9 Cf** Comfort	**10 Ic** Inclusion	**11 Wa** Wash	**12 St** Storage

The struggle between the efficiency and effectiveness of the workplace finds its ultimate stand-off in the consideration of the amount of space required. There is always a downward pressure from efficiency pushing against an upward pressure from effectiveness. Fortunately for the present and future workplace, there is a range within which both can live.

Space is measured in square metres or square feet per person, depending on the country in question (we shall use both) on an aggregated basis – all of the space divided by all of the people. Our aggregated measure includes the space in which people work, circulation space and all of the amenities and resources available. This has become increasingly relevant in the past decade with a move to less regular layouts within the overall space, where some work areas are highly concentrated some or all of the time (greater variance throughout the day being a more recent feature), allowing other, usually social, spaces to be provided. We cannot help, however, seeing it as the space in which each person works, applied consistently, as though each person were in a bubble, aloof and unconnected. We cannot visualize aggregated space.

It should be noted that, while most of the struggle in the modern age centres on the ability to provide enough space, it is also possible to provide too much, so that the overall effect isolates the occupants. It is the only Element where providing too much can be counter-productive.

Of course, space is not an isolated consideration when looking at the other Elements of the workplace. Greater provision of choice of setting and the freedom granted to employees to come and go, using the workplace as it suits, will affect how much space is provided overall and how this aggregates back to each individual. Other factors are also at play, including the configuration of the building in which the space is provided, and how intelligently the design is deployed. It is quite feasible to be gifted space in abundance and still waste it. In some countries, where space is cheap and little cost pressure exists, this problem proliferates.

For those seeking a metric, net internal area (NIA) usually suffices, which excludes things like lift (elevator) cores and toilets outside the areas covered by the lease – but every country has a national measurement code showing what is included and excluded from the total. When we talk about space within a building, we usually refer to NIA or its equivalent.

For many years in the UK, based on a combination of standards (real and imaginary), precedent and market-driven commercial caution, building systems, safety and core amenities have been designed and provided to support one person per 10 square metres (107 square feet) – often known simply as 'one in ten'. This metric was conceived in an age when all space was occupied in a generally uniform manner. If an organization wished to improve upon this efficiency, it would need to meet the cost of supplementing some or all of fire evacuation routes, fresh air, ventilation, heating and cooling systems, and toilets. Generally, any level of occupation density above this was reserved for rack-and-stack battery-farm workplaces such as contact centres.

If you were to swing a large toy cat with a reasonable amount of stuffed tail, it might create an area within a circle of approximately 6 square metres (65 square feet). That implies a radius of 1.38 metres (about 4 feet 6 inches). This would be the minimum amount of space per person acceptable, based on the provision of significant choice of setting and full permission for occupants to work when, where and how they choose. This is because 6 square metres looks very different when kitted out with rows of standard desks than in a more organic, agile setting.

This relates interestingly to the work of the American anthropologist Edward Hall in the 1960s,[42] who gave us the term 'proxemics' – theories around our use of space – and defined four distinct 'space bubbles': close, personal, social and public. Personal space extends from 0.45 to 1.2 metres (1 foot 6 inches to 4 feet), which is an area of up to 4.5 square metres (48.5 square feet). Setting aside obvious cultural variations in our view of space, this at least points to the idea that the toy cat experiment helps us avoid an uncomfortable invasion of our personal space in the workplace.

UK regulations (1992)[43] state that the minimum space per person is 11 cubic metres, which with a standard-height ceiling of 2.4 metres (7 feet 10 inches) would be 4.6 square metres (just under 50 square feet) – a shade over Edward Hall's definition of personal space. At this end of the scale, we are at emergency levels. Co-working centres often hit 6 square metres per person, given their commercial pressure to be profitable, the desire of customers to keep their costs down, and a greater focus on shared communal spaces. Clearly, however, expectations and standards in regard to how much space is deemed a minimum and how much is seen as sufficient vary between countries.

At the upper end of generosity, an allocation above 15 square metres (160 square feet) per person will appear gratuitous: it would separate the occupants to an extent

42   Edward Hall, *The Hidden Dimension* (repr. New York: Bantam Doubleday Dell, 1988).

43   "Workplace (Health, Safety and Welfare) Regulations 1992: Approved Code of Practice and Guidance", *Health & Safety Executive*, 2013, http://www.hse.gov.uk/pubns/books/l24.htm

verging on isolation. Any opportunity to create a sense of atmosphere will likely be lost. For some organizations, this may nevertheless be appropriate, and so while this book sounds a cautionary note, it does not claim that such a figure is specifically wrong.

It is quite possible to create a fantastic workspace with an aggregated 10 square metres per head (roughly 107 square feet). Well-structured buildings maximizing usable space and housing a relatively flexible workforce could see this pushed down to 8 square metres (86 square feet), the reverse of these factors increasing it to 12 square metres (130 square feet). The configuration of the building also influences the suitability of the space and therefore has an impact on the total, which is why retaining some flexibility at the outset is important.

Space also affects communication. Studies such as those in the late 1970s that yielded the Allen Curve[44] identified an exponential drop in the frequency of communication between engineers as their physical distance increased. Allen repeated the experiment more recently[45] and found the same to be true across *all* forms of communication. The practice of those developing software using the iterative methodologies of Agile Engineering are testimony to this, as mentioned earlier. Operating in 'scrums' or teams of eight to ten in close physical proximity, communicating frequently in non-hierarchical 'stand-ups' at whiteboards covered in tracking information and sticky notes, they are digital professionals using analogue tools and methods. This is not to deny the power of the digital workplace, explored earlier, to create new connections and relationships; it is more a case of teams working together on related tasks in physical space needing the benefit of close proximity. It is the social workplace in action.

It should be emphasized that the calculation of sufficient space occurs at the start of the process, at Brief stage or even before. It is a factor that needs to be considered, understood and committed to, and then the rest of the journey begins. It is an Element to agree, and then to take off the table.

The toy cat from the original experiment is still around, should anyone wish to borrow it to prove a point. Hopefully you will not have to.

---

44   Thomas J. Allen, *Managing the Flow of Technology: Technology Transfer and the Dissemination of Technological Information Within the R&D Organization* (Cambridge, MA: MIT Press, 1984).

45   Thomas J. Allen and G. Henn, *The Organization and Architecture of Innovation: Managing the Flow of Technology* (Burlington, MA: Butterworth-Heinemann, 2007).

CHOICE

1 **Da** Daylight		2 **Co** Connectivity

3 **Sp** Space	4 **Ch** Choice	5 **In** Influence	6 **Cn** Control	7 **Re** Refresh
8 **Se** Sense	9 **Cf** Comfort	10 **Ic** Inclusion	11 **Wa** Wash	12 **St** Storage

Nothing speaks of trust quite like allowing people choice. Even if that choice is limited, it still signals that within evident parameters, whether physical or time-based, it's up to you. The most genuine expression of a trusting approach to work is an organization that allows its people to work when, where and how they choose. Each of the three requires different things to be true to make it possible, and it often happens that organizations allow or enable only one or two of them. It requires an enlightened approach to management and people supported by a working environment and technology that enables choice. Of all of the Elements, it is choice that most requires a cultural contribution in order to be successful.

PERMISSION

It may seem obvious, but needs stating nevertheless, that choice requires both possibility and permission. It is pointless having a range of wonderful work settings if you are expected to be at a desk from 9 to 5 every day, and equally dim to be given the freedom to exercise choice but have access to only desks, offices and meeting rooms.

In this regard, much is made of what is incorrectly called 'presenteeism' (which means attending work when unwell), whereby managers believe they need to see their people to be sure that work is being done. It is a Taylorist, optimized view of work. There is a better expression for our purposes: 'panoptic management'. At the end of the 18th century, English philosopher Jeremy Bentham designed the Panopticon, a radical re-appraisal of the prison. Setting aside comic references to office life being akin to captivity, the prison was designed to minimize cost and increase the chances of rapid prisoner rehabilitation. Under the model, a single viewing station is able to cover all of the cells, so that a lone guard is able to keep check – or even no guard at all, since the prisoners could not see the guards and therefore would not know if they were absent. The theory was that the prisoners, believing they were being constantly scrutinized, would rehabilitate themselves more quickly. The idea may have its symbol in the 'all-seeing eye' that began its journey into ubiquity as the Eye of Horus, the ancient Egyptian sky god. It appears in Buddhism as the Eye of the World, and is even depicted as the Eye of Providence on the reverse of the Great Seal of the United States. As with the notion of panoptic management, the eye is both protector and conscience.

The exercise of choice in the workplace renders panoptic management almost impossible, and therefore is probably the single most important element in driving cultural change. It requires that individuals learn how to be managed, and to manage their teams, peer relationships and themselves differently.

For the purposes of this book, we need to assume that a degree of permission is granted: choice may be exercised. We should assume that the 'when' is resolved too, in regard to how flexible working operates within the organization, though in the physical workplace choice may function effectively without it. Even under a strict 9 to 5 regime, the choice of 'how' and 'where' might be possible. That said, the how and where are intrinsically related. The where often dictates the manner of choosing of how, and the how drives the requirements for different responses of where. As previously discussed, within most modern organizations, of whatever type, we spend around half our time in singular pursuits and half our time working with colleagues. There are often minor activities thrown in to create the required degree of over- complication, but activities such as 'learning' are subsets of individual or collective activity. If nothing else, this is a starting point.

BUILDING BLOCKS

The physical environment can guide the desired change. The creation of choice is often associated with 'activity-based' workplaces, an idea that has its roots in a 1985 paper by American architects Robert Luchetti and Phil Stone entitled "Your Office Is Where You Are".[46] In this scenario, a variety of shared work settings are created to meet the needs of all work tasks during a typical day, and the occupants are encouraged to move between them as needed. It is what many understand to be an 'agile' workplace, and hence the terms have become interchangeable. However, the provision of choice need not result in an activity-based workplace; it could be applicable to an altogether more traditional outcome too. In this way, the idea of choice continues to keep the Elemental Workplace above any steer towards a particular outcome.

Though perhaps equally obvious, it also needs stating that although the occupants of a workplace are 'at work', the choice of spaces needs to reflect both work and non-work activities. It would be overly simplistic to say that all non-work activity is play, as much of this is neutral and at times does not even qualify as activity. On the basis that every space beyond the typical desk should be able to support a range of uses, it minimizes the wastefulness of assigning spaces to a specific intended use.

---

[46]   Robert Luchetti and Philip Stone, "Your Office Is Where You Are", *Harvard Business Review*, Vol. 63 No. 2 (1985), p102-117.

The Elemental Workplace therefore contains a spectrum of work settings or space types to support a range of activities from the most quiet and focused at one end to the most interactive at the other, and includes those that are formal and informal, open and enclosed. They are divided into two types along this spectrum, 'primary' settings (that is, generally, desks) and 'alternative' settings (everything else: lounge, breakout, touchdown, formal and informal meeting, project space). It is a rare case within this book of a need for linearity! The spectrum should be as seamless as possible, given that the nature of our activities generally transitions rather than lurching from one isolated type to another. The approach of providing only desks and enclosed meeting rooms for many years denied a whole host of interactions in between. These work settings are the building blocks of our workplace that we shall need to consider at the Brief stage in regard to their number, their proportion to one another, and their performance. More is said on this in the chapter on "Comfort".

Interestingly, most environments irrespective of workstyle are best able to support choice when provided with roughly 14 seats to every 10 people. In a highly agile environment this would play out as seven desks of varying types (for focused and more team-based work) and a balance of seven seats in a range of alternative settings. When the ratio of desks to people is less ambitious, there might be (say) an aggregated eight desks to every ten people, but because of the higher likelihood of occupying a desk for longer periods of time, fewer alternative settings are needed and so this might become six seats for every ten people. In a one-to-one environment, where every person has a desk, meeting and training rooms and breakout spaces would still be needed and so this would reduce to four seats per ten people. Done properly, it is always 14 : 10.

A word on the humble desk. To date it has resisted all claims to its demise, and all attempts to force the pace of evolutionary obsolescence, principally because, in its simplicity, it works. It is the tardigrade (or 'water bear') of the workplace, able to survive all but the death of the sun. Yet all desks are not the same: some are better suited to open teamwork and some to quiet, individual work. That the desk is still the primary setting reflects its continuing dominance, but its form and performance can vary significantly.

Environments characterized by choice need to ensure that the work settings included provide a soft visual cue as to the intended use and behaviour. It could be the first such type of environment that people have worked in, and the settings could be puzzling. Those who plaster the settings in signage and do/don't protocols usually evoke a reaction to the compulsion, so it is better to choose features that inform and suggest, rather than instruct. A desk with raised sides and a task lamp, set away from the main circulation routes, will quietly let those approaching know that "I have my head down, I'm concentrating, I'll come and find you when I'm done." The whisper is sufficient.

TRIP HAZARDS

There are some things to look out for in the context of choice. First, a collected variety of settings alone does not guarantee success. In fact, a collection of poorly considered, ill-specified and badly designed settings in illogical locations will deliver a terrible workspace.

Those involved at the Brief stage need to be assured that this activity is vitally important. In some larger schemes, the choice of work settings will have been preceded by modelling of existing behaviours, but it is just as important to consider opportunities for behaviours that presently do not occur because the environment does not allow for them. Once again, there is a 50/50 split needed between data and opportunity.

Secondly, the variety of work settings should be manageable. There can be a tendency to over-develop the spectrum, considering minor changes in activity as a reason to specify another type. Too vast an array becomes incomprehensible to the occupants of the space. If there are more than three to five types of desk and more than seven to eight alternative settings, the process has probably gone too far and will need to be reined in.

Thirdly, the relationship between work settings is as important as the work settings themselves, so that adjacent spaces do not nullify one another. A huddle table for impromptu gatherings next to a bank of quiet desks is just going to annoy the users of both. It is often the result of lazy design, fitting shapes into spaces without considering the flow of the space.

Finally, choice will not succeed without the right day-to-day behaviour. An environment with opportunities for choice and permission to exercise it calls on the need for neighbourliness, as we considered in the chapter "Scope: The Social Workplace". Some choices may not be available, some may be used in a manner not intended, some may remain misunderstood. Being good to one another is in our blood; it comes easily to us. It is not a great deal to ask for a little freedom at work.

EXISTENTIAL THOUGHTS

Choice is an incredibly powerful Element, and vital to get right. It demands a lot of attention and consideration in the workplace design process, the rewards from which can be significant. Effective choice can deal with issues around inclusion, and it can resolve issues around difference, preference and control, particularly regarding noise. These are dealt with in their respective chapters.

Yet the freedom to choose should be a pleasure, not a burden. Some have complained that too wide a choice of setting imposes a tyranny in the workplace that mirrors the compulsion to be in the same seat between given times. Both are oppressive, overwhelming and stressful, and some people may just like to be told where to work. A step on from this idea is a restrictive palette in which the available choices are constrained by instruction and protocol to govern their usage, creating a degree of certainty that leaves us free to think of more interesting things. Though this is a minority view, it is worthy of note because it reminds us of the need for simple and intuitive design. No one should be burdened by choice.

We should also remember that electing not to exercise choice is itself a valid choice. We are always free not to choose – but it is better to do so in an environment where, one day, you may permit yourself to change your mind.

INFLUENCE

1 **Da** Daylight				2 **Co** Connectivity
3 **Sp** Space	4 **Ch** Choice	5 **In** Influence	6 **Cn** Control	7 **Re** Refresh
8 **Se** Sense	9 **Cf** Comfort	10 **Ic** Inclusion	11 **Wa** Wash	12 **St** Storage

Who designs the workplace? The process, in very simple terms, usually runs from visioning to Brief to design to construction to occupation. At each juncture, there are opportunities for those other than the small group running the project to get involved, have a say, specify a requirement, express a view or co-create an outcome. A higher degree of involvement at any juncture does not ensure a better outcome, but can potentially drive a greater sense of ownership and association vital to the change journey. At the end of a project, the rolling list of credits should be extensive.

Essentially, influence can be divided into three broad stages – pre-design, design and space-in-use. The **pre-design** stage is all about what is wanted, with a view to what it might look like and how it might function, but leaving the matter open to creative interpretation. Agreement is quite possible if the key components and characteristics are broad and general, such as those described in the earlier chapter "Why Create a Fantastic Workplace?" We can all broadly support, say, openness and transparency, or the creation of a social hub, even if we are not quite sure what that will end up meaning for us on a day-to-day basis.

The most difficult stage in which to explore wide involvement is **design**. This is where interpretations vary, tastes come into play and personal preferences conflict. It was once commonplace for items such as workstations to be chosen by vote, yet when five options were arrayed and the votes shared out between them, the outcome often resulted in a large majority opposing the selected installation. At scale, participative design becomes an incredibly difficult and sensitive challenge to manage. Very often, wide-ranging pre-design activities, funnelled into a small specialist team and then regularly played back at key stages for feedback and potential modification, produce a more generally agreeable outcome. It creates a sense of engagement and emotional connection without the risk of unnecessary tension. There are those who are not entirely comfortable with this angle, but this comes from an amalgamated experience of a variety of large-scale projects in various locations.

The influence that is of most interest within the Elemental Workplace occurs within the final stage, **space-in-use**. At the point of occupation, workspace rarely looks lived in, and has not been tested for functionality. It needs to look and feel lived in, and to work. This is the point at which the relationship between the space and its occupants begins, and it is highly unlikely to remain sterile. The possibility of influence, together with the permission to influence, needs to exist.

This can be achieved in four ways. First is the composition of the workplace, allowing the removal of some types of work settings and the addition of others, reflecting its evolving status as perpetual beta. Some work settings have a lovely habit of being successful in most guises and schemes. These include the diner booth – it is rare for more not to be called for at the expense of another setting type. The diner booth has been the star addition to the array of typical work settings in the past two to three decades. Changing patterns of work may also identify a requirement for settings not yet included.

The second consideration is arrangement, or how the settings relate to one another and the flow of work or people, allowing for re-arrangement as needed. For this, they need to be demountable and portable, particularly if lifts or stairs are involved. They are not sufficiently portable if oxy-acetylene torches are needed.

Thirdly, the way the settings are used, either individually or collectively, should enable alternative uses besides that originally intended. Design should have no ego in this regard. It was suggested in the chapter on "Choice" that each type of space should softly whisper its intended use – but, if one or more people decide that it is better suited for something else, as long as that occurs within the spirit of neighbourliness, that is fine. The design and arrangement of the work settings should also allow alternative usage. A design challenge worth adopting is to plan for each setting to have more than one evident use, to allow even greater freedom for occupants to choose.

Last comes enhancement, as in allowing the possibility of adding to the settings to change their use or character. Though this often means personalization (as opposed to decoration) at an individual level – the sort of challenge bemoaned by most facility managers – it could mean a team contributing to a shared space to add character and personality. Examples have included the display of awards or framed photos of each team member as a child, the creation of a library, or the addition of 3D installations relevant to the work being undertaken.

Opportunities for personalization are often proportional to the degree of choice of setting within the workplace. In environments where people move to use the spaces they need for a particular function, less time is spent at a regular desk, whether assigned or shared. The sensory stimulation afforded by the environment also comes into play, reducing the compulsion of the occupant to express their interests or personality in a particular space.

The arrangement and enhancement of work settings are the subject of research by a team led by Dr Craig Knight at the University of Exeter, who spent considerable time looking at the effects on productivity of enabling occupants to influence the design of their space.[47] The authors looked at lean (bare and functional), enriched (decorated with plants and pictures), empowered (allowing the individual to move the plants and pictures around) and disempowered (where the individual's design was redesigned by a manager) and found that for clerical tasks those working in enriched spaces were 17% more productive than those in lean spaces, but those sitting at empowered desks were 32% more productive than their lean counterparts, without any increase in errors. Enrichment can come from a variety of sources, more of which are explored in the "Sense" chapter. For this chapter, it is the empowerment that is interesting because it is influence in action, the ability and the permission.

The exercise of influence is healthy: as workplace creators we have to make it possible, and as workplace managers we must permit and welcome it. It is evidence that people are engaged and involved, that a relationship exists between the space and its occupants. It promises a purposeful future.

47 C. P. Knight and S. A. Haslam, "The Relative Merits of Lean, Enriched, and Empowered Offices: An Experimental Examination of the Impact of Workspace Management", *Journal of Experimental Psychology: Applied*, No.16 (2010), p158-172.

CONTROL

1 **Da** Daylight			**2** **Co** Connectivity
3 **Sp** Space	**4** **Ch** Choice	**5** **In** Influence	**6** **Cn** Control	**7** **Re** Refresh
8 **Se** Sense	**9** **Cf** Comfort	**10** **Ic** Inclusion	**11** **Wa** Wash	**12** **St** Storage

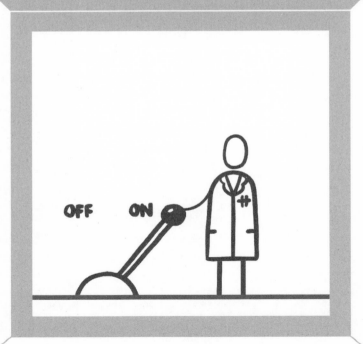

A workplace can often feel like an impersonal place in which we do not matter, where our own particular needs are simply there to be aggregated. The theory behind large-scale Milton Keynes-style planning and design works on the principle that the factors you may wish to control are so well thought through and implemented that personal awareness of something being amiss is rare, and therefore the need for localized control is minimized if not removed altogether. Yet this rarely works out in practice due to the differences between us. We are not an aggregated mass, or an average derived from it. We will always have a personal, individual need for control of our workplace.

Specific factors we may wish to control are thermal comfort (temperature, air velocity, radiant temperature from equipment, and humidity), lighting levels, and noise and the perception of noise (often referred to as psychoacoustics).

THERMAL COMFORT

Thermal comfort relates to the interplay between the design and effective operation of building systems on the one hand, and on the other the physical layout of the workplace and the orientation and location of the building. Generally, a temperature of 21-24°C (admittedly this range varies wildly around the world, and in different contexts) with a relative humidity of 40-70% (itself a wide range) will suffice for most sedentary office activities. However, we often find someone sitting in a puffa jacket adjacent to another in a singlet in the same conditions, both wishing they could do something about it. Interestingly (and worryingly), the UK's Health & Safety Executive states that the measure of thermal comfort in the workplace should be the number of people complaining about thermal comfort[48] – this assumes that people's voices can be heard, and are then taken seriously. The hierarchy of building to layout to systems can, however, be sensibly applied to the workplace, with as much segmentation and zoning as possible to allow local control. However, the volume of complaints should never be the measure of success of anything, as our (essentially British) 'mustn't grumble' indomitability suggests. There should either be a direct control available or easy access to someone with direct control and a willingness to use it. Of course, neighbourliness applies when occupying an area larger than your own domain – before turning the dial or asking someone to do so, a polite request is always appreciated.

LIGHTING

Our need for workplace lighting has changed with the kit we use on a day-to-day basis. General UK guidance sets a level of 500 lux (a measure only understandable by engineers) for office-related tasks, while acknowledging that working with computers can reduce the requirement to 300-500 lux. Invariably, however, the office is awash with light-emitting equipment, yet we still have to endure the headache-inducing fizzle of overhead fluorescent tubes, which is an outdated vestige from a time when we read papers and wrote memos by hand. What is needed is control over lighting levels – meaning a general level of 200-300 lux of preferably LED lighting across the general office space, supported by localized task-based lighting that suits the nature of the setting and the work being undertaken. Daylight, one of our key Elements, also needs some control. Depending on which way the external façade is facing, too much direct sunlight can be at times highly problematic and local blinds will be needed. It remains paradoxical that some of the best natural light we may experience needs to be entirely blocked for short periods of the day.

NOISE AND INTERRUPTION

This has been an issue ever since the workplace began to open up in the late 1980s (earlier if one counts the excellent *Bürolandschaft* experiments). There is noise we want and noise we do not want. Background 'buzz', the white noise from conversations we cannot untangle, can create a useful backdrop in an open environment, that is until one penetrating voice becomes discernible above the hum and we fixate upon it, being exposed to the wrong half of a conversation, allowing it to shatter our concentration. Hearing entails our ear and brain working together.

It is as much about how we perceive certain noises as the noise itself – the sound level accounts for only part of the annoyance. The degree to which we can become accustomed to background noise is still very much in debate, and there is considerable research underway into the notion that personality type has a role to play in how we process noise and its effect on our performance. Yet there are also the oft-raised benefits of overhearing conversations, promoting effective collaboration. You will have noticed throughout this book that there are a large number of areas of workplace design that reside in uncertainty.

The simple solution for many in an acoustically challenging environment is noise-reducing headphones, removing the sound we do not want to hear and replacing it with

---

48 "Managing Workplace Temperature," Health & Safety Executive, September 12, 2017, http://www.hse.gov.uk/temperature/thermal/managers.htm.

that we do. This always seems a pity, as though somehow the scheme has failed and let people down. It is almost as though we are clamping a private office to our head.

The work of Dr Nigel Oseland in association with Paige Hodsman has resulted in the DARE model[49] – Displace, Avoid, Reduce, Educate. The first three are effectively overlapping and complementary design considerations, in which a range of settings and permission to exercise choice (that is, avoid noise) will play a significant role. The final point relates to our behaviour – good neighbours respect and look out for one another. If we are behaving excellently to one another, there is no need for the code of conduct poster and the red and green flags on the desk. There may also be no need, either, for the DARE model, if we all behave that respectfully. Prevention succeeds, removing the need to search for a cure. This applies to all aspects of control: since we generally share workspace to one degree or another, the extent to which we require control varies from that of our neighbours. Consideration and choice in tandem have far-reaching benefits.

We need to distinguish between noise and interruption. A discipline called "interruptive science" looks at the effects of disruption on performance, offering the general rule of thumb that it takes 23 minutes to recover concentration after an interruption, according to the leading practitioner in the field, Gloria Mark.[50] These interruptions can be the result of a noise or a physical intervention (such as a tap on the shoulder), and are often used in arguments against more open environments. There should always be places available in which to work without fear of interruption, where the space itself visibly means "leave me alone".

It should also be noted, however, in keeping with the experiential nature of noise, that silence can be disturbing for some, too – whether that is a pure, stultifying, paralysing silence, or just a very low level of background noise that creates a situation in which people are nervous of speaking or moving for fear of being overheard by everyone around them. A blanket of silence can sometimes descend on a new workplace in which the occupants have recently moved from enclosed, cellular spaces to a shared, open environment, where new norms of behaviour have not had a chance to develop. In some instances, therefore, the challenge is not one of the original idea of DARE but of giving permission to make noise, or a re-stated DARE model that is "Demonstrate, Advocate, Relax and Engage".

The combination of localized control over thermal comfort, lighting, noise and interruption, along with an intelligently considered and well-designed choice of settings, is incredibly powerful. These things are also proportional – less of one requires more of another. However, it should not be assumed that one can be deployed to remove the need for the other. They can and should work beautifully together.

49 Nigel Oseland and Paige Hodsman, "Resolving Noise Distractions in the Workplace", in Alan Hedge (ed.), *Ergonomic Workplace Design for Health, Wellbeing and Productivity* (Boca Raton, FL: Taylor & Francis, 2017).

50 Kermit Pattison, "Worker, Interrupted: The Cost of Task Switching", *Fast Company,* July 28, 2008. https://www.fastcompany.com/944128/worker-interrupted-cost-task-switching

REFRESH

1 **Da** Daylight				2 **Co** Connectivity
3 **Sp** Space	4 **Ch** Choice	5 **In** Influence	6 **Cn** Control	7 **Re** Refresh
8 **Se** Sense	9 **Cf** Comfort	10 **Ic** Inclusion	11 **Wa** Wash	12 **St** Storage

Refreshment encompasses the reinvigoration of both physiology and spirit. Eating and drinking are, of course, essential physiological requirements. The time we spend in the workplace requires that we shall need to refresh, probably several times, and this applies to the overwhelming majority of those present. We all need it; we all need to do it. As we draw people to spaces where this happens, the *social* potential is therefore huge. Refresh space is invariably workspace as well as social space, supporting individual and group work, often creating work-oriented scenarios when starting from a social position – or vice versa. It can also be a meditative, solo space, somewhere to withdraw from the working environment. It requires the design of a catering offer (whether staffed or not) and a space, in harmony. In recent years there has also rightly been an increasing expectation of the provision of good-quality refresh facilities in the workplace. The potential to improve the workplace is significant – as of course is the potential to irritate, annoy, disappoint and in some cases actually cause harm.

PHYSIOLOGICAL NEED

This book does not need to delve deeply into the benefits of food and drink to the human body, but the design of the catering offer is as important as the design of the facilities themselves. There is no benefit from a superb café serving terrible food. We are, without doubt, better after we are refreshed. We think more clearly, are more social and make better decisions. Sometimes the benefit may be merely perceived, a placebo effect, to the degree that some have convinced themselves they cannot function without coffee in the morning.

The evidence of the benefit of eating and drinking the right things at the right time is everywhere. In much-publicized research in 2011, it was reported in a paper[51] in the *Proceedings of the National Academy of Sciences* that the sentencing passed down by Israeli judges was far more lenient after a refreshment break. The probability of a generous ruling declined from a peak of around 65% after a break to close to 0% just before the next break. Of course, this was not deemed to be the only causal factor, but was in the mix none the less. It has also been discovered through research by the universities of Cambridge and California[52] that the ability of a cheese sandwich to increase serotonin levels through the amino acid tryptophan present in the filling may help you when negotiating your pay, as it aids focus on matters of detail affecting your own interests. There are many other stories like this that underscore the need for a balanced, great-quality offer.

It is not the purpose of this book to delve into the finer points of menus, either, other than to say that in terms of drinks there is a clear expectation of good-quality bean-to-cup coffee and a range of leaf teas, and with food a balance between healthy and more (shall we say) standard fare. Much depends on whether the facilities are centralized or dispersed, as addressed below, and it will vary by geographical location and culture. Allied to all of this is needed product information – calories, fat, salt and sugar content as a minimum. We quite reasonably expect to be told what is in what we are consuming.

In terms of promoting wellbeing and enabling workplace occupants to make better decisions, there are ways to incentivize healthier options through what is and what is not offered in the first place, and then through promotions, pricing and health information. Do bear in mind that, if you offer pies and someone wants a pie, they will have a pie, so it is then pointless becoming frustrated over the eating of pies.

SOCIAL NEED

The social need is arguably just as strong as the physiological. It is resisted on a regular basis by those depositing crumbs in their keyboard, the self-anointed desk warriors for whom refresh is like grabbing a bottle from a water station in a half marathon. For many, taking a break from work to eat lunch is seen as slacking, a habit that belongs firmly in the past and is not commensurate with a dynamic, success-oriented present. This is, of course, bunkum.

Eating and drinking have been shrouded in ceremony and ritual in a myriad of unconnected cultures across the world for millennia. The *Cha Ching,* written by Lu Yu around the year 760 CE, during the Tang Dynasty, famously documents the Chinese tea ceremony. Taking afternoon tea still stirs the desire in organizations for downing tools and gathering in a social space to talk. Tactical serendipity or pure social joy, the experience is often found to be heart-warming. The tradition of *fika* (coffee break) is entirely commonplace in Swedish and Finnish workplaces, where coffee and tea are taken with colleagues (interestingly, rarely with senior management present); and in Turkey work often stops several times a day for tea and *simit* (a pastry). The practice has been slowly re-emerging in the UK, where, for example, *Financial Times* staff attend

51 Shai Danziger, Jonathan Levav and Liora Avnaim-Pesso, "Extraneous Factors in Judicial Decisions", *PNAS,* Vol. 108 No. 17, (2011) p6889-6892.

52 Molly J. Crockett, Luke Clark, Golmaz Tabibni et al., "Serotonin Modulates Behavioral Reactions to Unfairness", *Science,* Vol. 320, No. 5884, (2008) p1739.

the Thursday cake trolley, Instant Offices staff take turns to make tea for everyone at 3.30pm and Coffey Architects have adopted *fika*. The significance of this practice is that it demonstrates a willingness to take a break, and shows others the value of doing so in a world still in a desperate hurry. The phrase 'working on the pause' emerged some years ago, offered as a benefit of mobile technology – but the best thing to do on the pause is pause.

When considering a workplace transformation as a means of breaking down silos within the organization and encouraging people to work together more often, the social space can unlock the problem to a far greater extent than team adjacencies and any number of what-we-are-going-to-do-differently workshops. Well-designed and positioned facilities that people want to use (and can afford to use – more on this a little later) will ensure that this happens naturally. The communal refresh space should be the first feature on the plan, sited at a juncture where people will pass through it. The rest will simply happen.

In this vein, the Google café experience has been much talked about: free food served on small plates (a minor nod to wellbeing, unless you take two) in queues designed to hold you there for up to four minutes of potentially serendipitous exposure, then sitting on slightly-too-short benches so you might physically bump into someone. Other, longer-standing organizations have been offering free food in good-quality dining environments; it is just that Google liked to talk about it to create advocacy and reinforce its values. It added the catering experience to its ether.

BALANCING ACT

With all such facilities, centralized and localized, a place to consume is vital, with a focus on the social contribution. The design of a refresh space, particularly when staffed, requires that most of the other Elements be brought to bear: daylight and a view, a choice of comfortable settings, sensory stimulation, wifi connectivity, design for use by everyone, and nearby washrooms. It is an Elemental Workplace in microcosm. Dr Kerstin Sailer's fascinating PhD thesis,[53] based on a research institute in Germany, looked at the factors affecting the usage of a refresh space and found four, all intertwined: quality, location, spatial configuration and the chance of meeting interesting people – all heavily influenced by an Elemental approach.

In creating refresh spaces, there are a number of delicate balances to be struck.

High street or office?

Getting refresh right in the workplace is something that should be entirely possible, as influence and examples are all around us, from home to the high street and everywhere in between. The rise of the popularity of coffee shops on the high street helped drive the ability of the urban environment to sustain work activity beyond the office, and showed us that with wifi, toilets, power, and food and drink we can work anywhere, within reason. In part it helped fuel the early proliferation of co-working spaces, where the benefits of the café in terms of ambience and aesthetic were matched with a vastly improved working experience

---

53   Kerstin Sailer, "A Tale of Two Coffee Cultures", *spaceandorganization*, May 6, 2013, https://spaceandorganization.org/2013/05/06/a-tale-of-two-coffee-cultures/

and none of the irritations, notably from other customers not associated with the work being done, un-ergonomic furniture, and the need to take everything with you to the toilet. The balance lies in drawing the best ideas and influences from the high street and discarding the worst effects and practices, while maintaining a distinct and relevant function and identity relative to the workplace in which it is being created.

Staffed or self-service?

Generally, centralized facilities enable a far greater opportunity for providing a whole-building social focal point, and for providing a high-quality staffed facility and offer. They also tend to be more effective and successful the closer they are positioned to a reception area, where they can cater for both employees and visitors in an experience akin to the high street.

There are no rules or guidelines attached to what type of refresh facilities a workplace should have, and so a rough rule of thumb is offered here, even if just as a starting point for discussion. If the workplace is either out of town (as in, nothing reasonable is nearby) and/or has more than 200 people wherever it is sited, it would seem reasonable to have a dedicated staffed catering facility offering food and drink. Below this number, and/or in a central urban location, it may not be necessary to provide a dedicated staffed facility, albeit kitchenettes and the opportunity to make good-quality drinks and prepare or reheat food would be a minimum capability.

Expectations have been changing and this rule of thumb is becoming challenged to an increasing degree. It is also recognized that organizations may benefit by retaining staff in the building and not having them waste time traipsing along the high street in search of food. There are many more creative variants on a café offer available too, avoiding the need to create a full kitchen facility with its plant, extract and preparation area requirements, such as the 'soup-and-panini' style café. The figure of 200 people may need to be revised.

If the workplace does not allow much space at all for refresh facilities yet there is a desire to bring people together, refreshment can be taken directly to workplace occupants. The reinstatement of the tea trolley may just be the means. A traditional squeaky wheel can always be retro-fitted for authenticity, so we can hear it coming – we are all 'Pavlov's dogs'.

Subsidized or market price?

Inevitably the matter of subsidy arises when catering facilities are considered. Most organizations will work with a degree of subsidy, which may vary from the full cost of the materials, facility, labour and profit (as in a high street outlet) to almost zero. The question as to the 'right' level is often asked, but the only right level is the one that is appropriate for your organization. There are benefits to free food and drink, just as there are likely repercussions if people do not value the offer without a financial contribution. However, overall, generosity matters. Whether it takes the form of free tea and coffee, subsidized breakfasts and lunches, free fruit or the 'mass offer' such as free muesli, it has come to be expected and therefore its absence is generally seen as poor form.

Quite how many cups of fresh-brewed coffee and leaf tea went into the writing of this book is staggering.

SENSE

1 **Da** Daylight				2 **Co** Connectivity
3 **Sp** Space	4 **Ch** Choice	5 **In** Influence	6 **Cn** Control	7 **Re** Refresh
8 **Se** Sense	9 **Cf** Comfort	10 **Ic** Inclusion	11 **Wa** Wash	12 **St** Storage

A workplace plays to the senses. This is not something that can be avoided, and so needs to be understood and addressed. If we assume that taste is satisfied by the crushed avocado on sourdough toast with a poached egg at the reception café, it leaves a craving for stimulation of sight, sound, smell and touch. The original idea in the earliest post on the Elemental Workplace was simply colour, but the thinking has moved on to encompass the full sensory palette. Everywhere we turn, it is a bombardment. When we start to consider space in this manner, we open up a range of possibilities – and, once again, the possibility of getting it wrong.

We may never attain in the workplace the emotional impact of Stendhal's Syndrome (hyperkulturemia), in which the great French writer fainted at the sheer multi-sensory splendour of Florence in the early 19th century, but we are innately drawn to beauty and are stimulated by it. Not absolutely everything needs to make a specific functional contribution; some things serve simply to prompt our imagination. It therefore needs to be recognized that, in their own way, such things are still functional.

Beyond the (occasional) wonder of the sweep and curve of the external building form, the architecture of interior spaces is a restricted playpen; yet, though scale limits form, it does not restrict impact. In response we must consider how we think about and use colour, texture, sound and scent.

COLOUR

Much has been said and written about colour. From 1666, when Sir Isaac Newton split white light into the colour spectrum using a prism, to the quackery that was current at the time when Stendhal was passing out on Tuscan streets, through to photobiology (the scientific study of the effects of light on living organisms), a variety of claims have been made about the power of colour to impact our thoughts, moods and behaviour. There are stories of a blue bridge (Blackfriars in London) stemming the flow of suicides and of passive pink calming violently disruptive prison inmates, amid claims that yellow attracts our attention, while red creates excitement and intensity. All of this of course ignores the cultural significance of certain colours and tones – white, for instance, the tone of purity in the West, is the tone of mourning in the Far East. It remains an area lacking in scientific rigour, so any claims in interior design to be prompting an outcome through the use of a particular colour should be handled with care.

Nevertheless, colour is important. The dominant trend for the past decade has been minimalism, paring back colour in favour of white and pale shades of grey with tiny bursts of accent. The dominance of 'greige', best encapsulated by the paint manufacturer Farrow & Ball's 'Elephant's Breath', has created some spectacularly uninteresting and unstimulating but rather calming environments. Colour is a property of the brain, not of light, and so the context (what else is going on around it) is vital – something not always considered by marketers when agonizing over the Pantone shade of a logo. Leaving aside the excessive claims of interior designers, the tasteful and cohesive use of colour within space has the power to provoke, inspire and motivate – and it need not cost much more than white. The Elemental Workplace is filled with daylight and colour, but has no expectation that the shades used will make anything beneficial happen for you. If they do, that is amazing.

TEXTURE

The cloudburst of novelty that is said to have occurred when Google first installed a slide in an office served to herald a little-discussed aspect: the ability for occupants of a space to physically and consciously interact with it, beyond simply sitting at a desk. Such features, spreading into the trend for other installations straight out of the playroom, lifted workspace out of its two-dimensional state in which people and space had little or no relationship. The annoyance they also created is beginning to bite, but we are left with an important consideration: that a workspace should encourage us to touch, to interact, to relate. Surfaces and installations should invite unprompted movement towards them. For example, the 'rope houses' installed at media company Sky Central in West London beckon to be strummed like a harp as you move through them. Create flat, feel flat. Avoid flat.

SOUND

Sound in the workplace is rarely considered and seldom features beyond very small office environments where everyone can agree on what they wish to listen to, or someone is unfortunately dominant enough to prevail. When people think of sound they think of music and 'muzak'. It is common to have music in the form of radio played in manual environments, but music in a larger office where more focused, cerebral activities occur (and people need to speak to each other and on the telephone) often polarizes opinion. Yet it may not always be about music. An experimental installation in the small lobby area at the Centre for Creative Collaboration in London (now closed, sadly) featured stringed instruments that would respond to movement sensors, thereby playing a subtle yet unique piece for every person moving through the space. It was intriguing and beautiful.

Sound used sparingly and creatively, therefore, may inspire. It needs to be handled with great care, however, as sound for some is noise to others. It can cause the same negative reaction as some of the disturbances mentioned in the chapter on "Control". There is no rule or guideline that dictates when one passes into the other. It is a matter of neighbourliness once again.

SCENT

How does your workplace smell? It depends much of the time on what is being reheated in the microwave, but yesterday's chicken bhuna might not be the only means by which olfactory systems are stimulated in the workplace – and that is beyond the 'forest glade' mist coating you get every ten minutes in the washroom. From the pumping of the smell of newly baked bread or freshly brewed coffee in retail outlets – designed to draw in customers and create a better mood – to just-created chocolate chip cookies on a crack-of-dawn Midwest Express flight (interestingly, this was originally the result of a cost-cutting exercise), the allure of the right scent at the right time is powerful. The 'brand stations' throughout the offices of Estée Lauder in London, as you can imagine, create a fragrant journey through the organization's purpose, while encouraging deeper breathing and a calm that stimulates thought.

All of this is because our olfactory bulbs are connected to our limbic system, which governs emotion and behaviour, and prompts 'associative learning', where we connect a smell to a particular event and this creates a response. Scientifically, a pleasant smell can put us in a better mood, which makes us potentially more creative and productive. This is why a newly created office where everything is straight out of the factory has an appealing impact, an experience often associated with a new car given the confined space in which it is experienced. Of course, care is required as this can have a detrimental effect too, the smell of curly fax paper and typewriter ribbons creating a negative association in those old enough to recall them.

SENSORY INCLUSION

Supporting the manner in which the human being was designed to function, the sensory works best in coherent combination. The senses combine to create meaning and metaphor that help us to navigate our way through and understand space. Help is required to get each – and the balance – right. It certainly need not be a high-cost contribution, but an Elemental Workplace recognizes our sensory needs and responds.

A final word of caution. This is effectively a 'twin chapter' with that on Inclusion. Not all human senses function in the way the operating manual intended. When planning a workplace, while we need to consider the impact of the full range of senses as we understand them, we also need to think through the potential effect on those for whom the impact could be non-existent or problematic. It is a delicate balance.

Moving beyond the five senses known to most of us, convincing arguments can be made for there being seven senses, perhaps more. Considerable work is being done in this area by Steve Maslin and his associates at Building User Design.[54] He expresses them in terms of their technical form – visual, auditory, olfactory, gustatory, tactile (taking account of the five with which we are familiar) – and then interestingly includes vestibular (the system governing balance and orientation, mostly found in the inner ear) and proprioceptive (the system governing position and movement, found in muscles and tendons). Steve's work focuses on ensuring that the brain has a sensory diet it can cope with, without triggering hypersensitivity. The overall message in this regard is therefore that we need to stimulate and motivate through sensory design, but pay heed to what that implies in terms of creating an inclusive environment. It is not an invitation to a free-for-all.

---

54 Steve Maslin, "Designing for Inclusion: Designing for Mind and Body," *SlideShare*, October 13, 2014, https://www.slideshare.net/maggieprocopi/design-for-mind-and-body-wpt-for-pdf

COMFORT

1 **Da** Daylight				2 **Co** Connectivity
3 **Sp** Space	4 **Ch** Choice	5 **In** Influence	6 **Cn** Control	7 **Re** Refresh
8 **Se** Sense	9 **Cf** Comfort	10 **Ic** Inclusion	11 **Wa** Wash	12 **St** Storage

Comfort is an entirely personal experience, and invariably elusive. For this reason, this chapter looks at how we create the *conditions* for comfort through the specification, design and arrangement of work settings. We started developing our idea of the work setting spectrum in the chapter on "Choice" but paused to allow a fuller development in this chapter.

Definitions of comfort often emanate from the area of health care and recovery, and extend to all aspects of personal comfort. Considerations of environmental comfort such as thermal, lighting, noise and distraction are dealt with in the chapter on "Control", leaving us here to focus on the comfort associated with physical work settings. It has ergonomics at its heart – best defined as "the practice of designing products, systems, or processes to take proper account of the interaction between them and the people who use them".[55]

WORK SETTING SPECIFICATION

There are three stages to effective work setting specification.

First, **listening** to the occupants and studying existing patterns of behaviour, identifying what is working and what could be improved upon. This includes gathering quantitative data on occupancy levels and work types. Data also includes stories: what actually happens and why. These help to give meaning and colour to the quantitative data. This can take time, as space and trust are needed for stories to unfold.

Secondly, an **exploration** of opportunities for doing things differently or better. Most people do not know what they can have, unless they have seen something elsewhere

---

55 "Human Factors and Ergonomics," *Wikipedia*, accessed September 2, 2017, https://en.wikipedia.org/wiki/Human_factors_and_ergonomics

that has sparked their curiosity. Taking people through this process requires a degree of what may be termed 'dreamscaping': exploring how working life might be in an ideal environment. It may include visits to recently completed schemes to consider what may work and what may not when applied at home. The flattery of copying in this regard is not wrong, provided it is duly acknowledged and contextualized.

Thirdly, the **definition** of the building blocks, the settings that will be deployed to enable choice to be exercised. This is all too often an aspect of the Brief phase that is hurried through or treated with undue disregard even by experienced designers. Layout work cannot start without this activity having been completed. It includes consideration of the purpose of the setting, the quantity and proportion to be included in the scheme, and its performance criteria, including technological support and capability. At this stage, we also establish likely relationships with other space, to help with the arrangement stage, below. The degree of comfort required is itself also one of the performance criteria. It is worth remembering that low levels of comfort where the shortest possible stay is intended might be a legitimate design objective. The aesthetic qualities will come later. Each setting needs to be defined, yet hopefully avoiding awkward, fanciful or instructive names (the last place anyone ever had a great idea was in the 'Brainstorm Room'). Everyone should intuitively understand what each setting is and what it is for. Care needs to be taken in this regard for the change journey: we are creating a workplace, not a scene from *Alice in Wonderland*. If using names is too great a temptation, keep them simple and relevant. As established in the chapter on "Influence", a change of use in situ may make the name redundant.

These three stages should result in an effective range of well-specified work settings able to support work performed today and create opportunities for changes in work style in future. They now need to be designed.

WORK SETTING DESIGN

At this stage, each work setting is a specification and a shape on a space plan, no more. It is at this juncture that form and function slug it out. It is an old battle fought anew in every scheme.

The expression "form follows function" comes from the 1st-century BCE Roman architect Marcus Vitruvius Pollio (the model, due to his love of proportion, for Leonardo Da Vinci's "Vitruvian man"), who stated in his book *De Architectura* that all things we create must be solid, useful and beautiful. The modern revival of the phrase – correctly stated in this case as "form ever follows function" – was by the American architect Louis Sullivan (1856-1924).[56] He stated, rather lyrically, that, "Whether it be the sweeping eagle in his flight, or the open apple-blossom, the toiling work-horse, the blithe swan, the branching oak, the winding stream at its base, the drifting clouds, over all the coursing sun, form ever follows function, and this is the law."

Sadly, the law is not much applied, and is rarely enforced. The pervading design aesthetic of the past decade, encompassing cafés, restaurants, hotels and offices, has been the overwhelmingly industrial 'workshop chic' with its tendency to exposed brick, reclaimed timber, flaking plaster, furniture from the garden shed and – the epitome of the style – the filament lightbulb, with its flex dangled across the ceiling.

---

56 Louis Sullivan, "The Tall Office Building Artistically Considered," *Lippincott's Monthly Magazine*, No 57 (1896) p403-409.

If only it were as simple as "we found it like this" – but in many instances it is awkwardly reverse-engineered into space that was finished, clean and comfortable, creating something just a little embarrassing, the 'Dad dancing' of workplace. Such environments follow the simple adage that if it looks as though it will be uncomfortable, it probably will be.

Sullivan's law boils down to ergonomics. However, compliance with ergonomic regulations is absolutely no guarantee of comfort. This puts form and function in eternal, seismic and potentially unresolvable opposition, at least until the design industry chooses to close the gap. It has to choose. Our role is to ensure that the design process is managed so that where work settings are being designed for construction as bespoke items, or when readily available furniture is being specified, checks are conducted on availability and ease of adjustability, back support, levels of acoustic privacy, ease of positioning, and ease of support for the use of technology. The aesthetic need not be set in opposition to the aim of comfort. With a little application, form and function can be intertwined, even become one idea, one objective, one outcome.

As mentioned throughout this book, the use of the installations should be as intuitive and simple as possible. Our understanding of them should be intrinsic, and adjustments to suit ourselves should be possible and easy. Ideally, comfort should be immediate, without training or instruction manuals.

WORK SETTING ARRANGEMENT

The arrangement of our well-specified and designed building blocks must reflect the flow of work, people and knowledge. It takes understanding and thought and is all too frequently completed in isolated disregard of both the specification and design of work settings.

The clues are always in the data, but are often either overlooked in favour of general design and industry trends – the drive towards collaborative spaces at the expense of all others being a regular culprit – or are dictated by the shape of, and available space within, the building envelope. Or, of course, both.

This is the point at which comfort bites. For each setting to work, its relationship with others must be perfect, or the function of each is compromised. Common failings include quiet, focused spaces on main circulation routes, and a particular personal *bête noire*, the positioning of adjacent open meeting spaces so that they nullify one another.

BEHAVING COMFORTABLY

Assuming we are able to ensure the conditions for comfort within the work settings specified, designed and arranged, there are still behavioural issues that can help. As managers of facilities, we can provide information and guidance where intuition ends. As occupants we can pay attention to what we are told or given, and do our bit – we can still slouch and slump in the most ergonomically designed task chair.

The solution to commonly experienced problems associated with sedentary workplace practice is invariably to follow guidance on the best use of the equipment, furniture and fixtures provided (requesting it if it is not provided) and to regularly move around, however comfortable the installations. This once again emphasizes the importance of choice. Your backside is a contributor, not a destination.

Comfort properly considered and applied, enabling intuitive or well-informed behaviour, is ideally a state we should never be aware of; it should just *be*.

INCLUSION

1 **Da** Daylight				2 **Co** Connectivity
3 **Sp** Space	4 **Ch** Choice	5 **In** Influence	6 **Cn** Control	7 **Re** Refresh
8 **Se** Sense	9 **Cf** Comfort	10 **Ic** Inclusion	11 **Wa** Wash	12 **St** Storage

A fantastic workplace should be fantastic for everyone. The moment, however, that we begin to talk about inclusion, our path is surfaced with eggshells. It is a sensitive area for good reason, that being for many decades we were not very good at considering the needs of everyone when designing and operating the workplace. The base point is lower than probably all of the other 11 Elements. Of course, the issues apply to society as whole, not just the workplace, so we are looking well beyond the confines of our subject area.

In terms of workspace specifically, people should not have to declare their personal circumstances or preferences in order for the workplace itself to enable them to take a full and active part. The space should simply allow everyone to access, use and depart without cause for drawing undue attention, or needing to make a specific request. The starting position must be that no one wants to be considered to have 'special needs' but that all special needs have been factored into the design thinking.

First, we have to comply. Construction and workplace design are governed by a host of regulations, most notably in the UK in Part M of the Building Regulations "Access to and use of Buildings".[57] Essentially, this is focused on physical disability. However, inclusion in this regard goes much further, as explored below. Next, we have to do much, much better. The Regulations are a safety net, a checklist of things that should be done. Also, compliance often takes an itemized approach to its subject matter,

---

[57] "The Bulding regulations 2010," HM Government, 2010, https://www.gov.uk/government/uploads/system/uploads/attachment_data/file/540330/BR_PDF_AD_M1_2015_with_2016_amendments_V3.pdf

rarely considering how those pieces come together and what the overall effect might be – all of the parts work, but the whole thing fails. When a situation is defended on the grounds that it is compliant, it merely means that it has achieved the minimum necessary. That is not a standard that the Elemental Workplace aspires to in this regard. We need to thoroughly design for the senses, the mind, the body and our orientation – that is, for the way we are and the way we choose to live.

Considerations of 'the way we are' include the degree to which we are able-bodied or restricted in our physical capabilities; the degree to which we are able-minded or restricted in our mental capabilities (and fortunately, with the rise of stress-related conditions, mental health is now being taken far more seriously in work-related situations); whether we have conditions such as autism, dyslexia, dyspraxia or ADHD; and our age, gender and personality.

In terms of the way we choose to live, considerations also include our sexuality and our religious beliefs. Each of these factors generates a workplace design response, in general or specific terms.

Susan Cain's 2012 book *Quiet: The Power of Introverts in a World That Can't Stop Talking*[58] shows that new focus can often be brought to bear on workplace matters with a well-argued case. Its popularity resulted from a raised awareness from many that their tendency to shun face-to-face social interaction in the workplace was at odds with a drive to have people work together and the creation of spaces that allowed or even forced this. It brought forth a silent cheer from millions of those preferring the tranquillity of solitude: however true the clarity of division between the extrovert and introvert (despite the tendency of most to oscillate at different times, in a more 'ambivert' manner), they can now seek spaces and settings that suit.

Shortly afterwards, Susan founded Quiet Revolution, an organization focused on rolling back the trend towards openness in workplace architecture in favour of space for focus and contemplation. A considered choice of settings once again resolves much of this. It does not stop the emotive and sensationalist critique of more open environments. A common thread of criticism of the open office is that organizational dysfunction is blamed purely on the physical environment, as its tangibility creates a simple target, while omitting to mention other possible contributors. These might include redundant command-and-control management structures, mistrust, increasingly unrealistic expectations of performance, the invasion of every corner of our lives by the technology that was once promised to set us free, the unrelenting demand to do more/to change/to progress/to be seen to be doing something useful, and the ephemeral nature of achievement, in which each triumph has only a short half-life, leading to a constricting lack of opportunity.

Our response needs to consider the way the workplace is designed. The space needs to be simple and intuitive, allowing access and movement, avoiding obstacles, removing doubt and guesswork, creating clear contrast, without features or installations that might create anxiety, not skewed to either gender, tolerant and inviting, with a working balance of aesthetics and functionality.

---

58 Susan Cain, *Quiet: The Power of Introverts in a World That Can't Stop Talking* (New York: Crown Publishers, 2012).

Designing to a perceived demographic (as often occurs in technology environments, for example) must be avoided, as that can change quickly.

Secondly, we need to consider the way we *suggest* the space is designed. The space itself will speak to us; it will prompt our understanding of how it may be used. We need to consider the positioning of installations and their relationships, allowing time for occupants to relate to them. If they are over-designed, difficult to access, or unduly distracting, then they will cause concern and anxiety.

Thirdly, we need to consider the way we are *told* the space is designed. The signage and instruction we offer has a language: visual, symbolic and spoken. It has a tone and a temperature. It either invites us in or tells us to get lost. It either tells us we are trusted or wags a threatening finger. Very often signage is deemed necessary because of a shortcoming in the way we suggest the space is designed – that is, we have to say something because the message from the space itself is garbled. If we find ourselves needing signage, something else in the design has generally failed. The perfect workplace design needs no signage at all.

We also need to bear in mind that certain Elements advocated in this book may be problematic for some. We have already mentioned how daylight can present a problem. A further element – choice – can be brought into play to alleviate this by providing settings that will enable safety and comfort. As is becoming apparent on our path through the Elements, a choice of well-specified, well-designed, and well-arranged work settings is often the answer to so many workplace issues.

An inclusivity review of the workplace design at every stage is an excellent practice to adopt, in which the broadest range of scenarios is considered.

The strapline of the Elemental Workplace since its origination in 2014 has been: "Everyone deserves a fantastic workplace." It may seem implicit, but that really does mean absolutely everyone.

WASH

1 **Da** Daylight				2 **Co** Connectivity
3 **Sp** Space	4 **Ch** Choice	5 **In** Influence	6 **Cn** Control	7 **Re** Refresh
8 **Se** Sense	9 **Cf** Comfort	10 **Ic** Inclusion	11 **Wa** Wash	12 **St** Storage

One of the strongest value signals that can be sent to the occupants of a building is to create a fantastic washroom experience. To clarify, they are called washrooms because we expect their function to be broader than simply the water closet or urinal. We might at a stretch include shower facilities within the definition, although in some buildings this is simply not physically possible.

Fix the washrooms; fix them now. Though this book has been clear on the need to fix the technology first, in second place are the washrooms. If in any doubt, fix them and see what happens, what reaction is created and what stories are told. There is sanity in paying attention to the sanitary. It tells us much about our relationship with our employer, what they think of us and consequently what we think of them. As they are the only area covered by this book in which work does not actually take place (unless, of course, you take your phone with you), their importance as a barometer of value is of even greater importance. It says, if you think and care about this space, then you care deeply. Your visitors are probably going to want to visit your washrooms too. Besides the reception and perhaps a meeting room, it's one of the few areas of your workplace they will probably see.

As for inclusion, the legal requirements in most countries extend in the main to sufficiency. We need to assume for the purposes of this discussion that we are compliant. For many of the workforce, that is where the experience ends. But it is actually where the experience should begin. We also regularly contend with the fact that the washrooms are often outside our space, and are the responsibility of a landlord. It is expected that a dialogue with the landlord exists, and that irreconcilable differences have not yet been cited. This is never a reason to ignore the washrooms; there is always an arrangement to be made that benefits both parties. The investment is not in the asset, but in the people using the asset.

There is an element of sanctuary in a visit to the washroom, as it is away from the workplace, a permitted other space; there is a degree of escape involved. There is no expectation to answer the phone, respond to email, even talk to the person next to you at the basin. It is a place where silence is permitted, accepted, even encouraged. We are welcome in our own thoughts. You also never quite know who is behind the locked cubicle door.

We invariably want a facility that has been recently decorated and is in a good state of physical repair, and is regularly cleaned (though taking care not to overdo this and prevent access – a fairly critical consideration). It must be warm enough not to induce anaphylactic shock when posterior touches seat, and decked with sufficient supplies so you do not have to text a colleague to roll a fresh one under the door. There must be locks on the doors where the screws have not been wrenched from their MDF dust pockets, and a coat hook on the back of the door; female washrooms need sanitary bins in each cubicle. There must be soap that leaves all known layers of skin intact, and hot water for hygienic hand washing (albeit in some countries the latter is not deemed necessary). Visitors should be able to choose a preferred hand-drying option; there is a huge debate still raging between paper towels made from recycled materials and low-energy yet earth-shatteringly-noisy hand driers. It must be light enough for us to see ourselves clearly and (dare it be said) even flatteringly in a mirror without scratches and cracks. There should be bag hooks beneath the sinks, both in the male and female outlets.

The space must be well ventilated and contain some form of regular air freshener so that we have no need to disconnect our olfactory senses entirely on entry.

A word on 'super-loos' is needed here. By this we mean individual self-contained washrooms that are gender-independent. They became fashionable as developers of speculative buildings sought to maximize the rentable area of their buildings by minimizing the non-rentable cores, understanding that they could legally get away with fewer washrooms if they were shared. The practice is relatively commonplace in many countries, particularly in Scandinavia. A decision on whether to provide washrooms that are gender-independent or those designated by gender often evokes a passionate response. For the purposes of inclusion, the former would be preferred – yet patterns of usage often lead them to be regarded negatively. In reality, both are required. To achieve this, the overall provision has to exceed statutory regulations. Typically, a 'disabled' washroom provision is included with a building to the minimum standard required. However, they should not be considered in this manner – they should be regarded as washrooms usable by everyone, designed and specified accordingly and provided generously. Invariably, a reliance on the landlord's provision of washrooms will be inadequate and they will need to be supplemented.

Fix the washrooms; fix them now.

STORAGE

1 **Da** Daylight				2 **Co** Connectivity
3 **Sp** Space	4 **Ch** Choice	5 **In** Influence	6 **Cn** Control	7 **Re** Refresh
8 **Se** Sense	9 **Cf** Comfort	10 **Ic** Inclusion	11 **Wa** Wash	12 **St** Storage

With the dream of the paperless office came the wish for the storage-free office. Where there was paper, there were inevitably rows of manila filing cabinets in which the paper was left to softly ochre at the edges, often seen as the essence of the stupor of the clerical workplace: the "dust from the walls of institutions, finer than flour" (from Roethke's poem) building over years of sloth on their static form. There has always been something fundamentally miserable about storage cabinets. They have invariably been stuffed with things we decided to retain because we were not sure if we might need them, all the while knowing we probably never would. We awaited their demise.

At least, that was how we once saw it. Storage is having a renaissance.

The modern age of wellbeing has given storage new meaning and purpose. The more we include wellbeing in our daily working lives, the more 'stuff' we bring: gym bags, cycling gear, various pairs of shoes. In addition, our increased mobility in office space has generated a need for a secure place for our valuables and items of kit. We need safe storage for our work stuff and our personal stuff, but rarely is this stuff made of paper. There are four broad areas of storage for us to be aware of.

The **locker** has in many instances taken over from the pedestal filing cabinet. In all but the one-to-one workplace, it is the secure vestibule for our purses, wallets, gadgets, a pair or two of shoes (admit it) and myriad other items that used to line the bottom of its predecessor. The contents of a locker are also dependent upon the other Elements. If you cannot get a good cup of tea or coffee and so need to bring your own, or if there are no hygiene supplies in the washrooms, then your personal storage will be full of stuff that really need not be there. The idea with lockers is to make them big enough – a minimum of 450mm (18 inches) cubed – with a good-quality coded lock (the keys will always get lost, and it will be the day that the person with your spare is on holiday). Better still, be over-generous: remove the pain and irritation to allow focus on the amazing things created in the workplace. A decent-sized locker is an indicator of 'sweating the small stuff'. If the amount of space is insufficient to put your personal effects in when you arrive, and to pack away your business things when you leave, no amount of vision statements and grand proclamations will make up for the fact that you have been annoyed by your workplace twice a day, at a minimum.

Pedestals are still in business. Where a one-to-one environment is created and the organization's people levels are stable, they still serve a purpose and disappear under the desk. What they do not do, however, is enable a change to a more flexible, mobile environment in future if this is desired as they tether an individual to a specific desk under which their stuff is stored. The switch from pedestal to locker never works well: it symbolizes (but does not actually entail) loss and can appear petty, even when the capacity is the same. It would always be recommended that lockers be introduced at the outset regardless of workstyle today as beneficial future-proofing.

Secondly, the humble **filing cabinet**, dour symbol of a slow demise? Not now. The gym bag, more shoes, merchandise and marketing materials, among other things, have replaced the serried rows of foolscap ring binders, actual physical things of varying shapes and sizes. We used to do filing audits, measuring the linear length of papers stored on end, planning to replicate the amount stored less a minor target for a little efficiency. A visual check and a sensible allocation should be sufficient as the basis for design. As a starting point, a linear metre (40 inches) per person for a standard working-height cabinet can help planning.

At the appropriate height, storage allied with internal planting also makes an architectural contribution to workspace, to prevent it becoming a sea of desks. It can break up space, direct and channel, while still performing a useful function. There are few other installations that can do this and remain useful. Trust can be strengthened by the symbolism of leaving the keys in the doors for self-organization; it can be an incredibly powerful complement to an approach that treats people as adults. There is, after all, something rather dismal about allocating storage cabinets.

Thirdly, storage or hanging space for **coats** is often an afterthought too – or not even a thought at all until the first downpour. Like the filing cabinet, the jacket on the back of the chair has come to symbolize a bygone age. It was the sign of being present when temporarily absent. There are countless stories of keeping a spare jacket in the office to pop on the back of a chair, teams taking it in turns to cover for one another.

Yet the coat cupboard is also a place of dark secrets. In a world of increasing transparency, it retains a mystical charm. Actually, it is usually full of unwanted or forgotten items that were too large for the filing cabinets. The cyclists usually have their week's shirts hanging therein. When coats are stored, they take on the personality of the wet waxed cotton jacket of the wearer who owns several dogs. In the workplace, there is little wrong with a plentiful supply of free-standing coat stands, the cost of which is comparatively minor. They hold no secrets.

Fourth and last is **off-site storage**, so often the easy option when it is difficult to decide what to keep. It allows materials to vanish, possibly forever, without anyone taking the responsibility of disposing of something that may just be required. There are few off-site storage systems that are managed effectively. Scrutinize what is stored, enforce destruction dates and apply these policies rigorously. Since marginal costs are tiny, such systems proliferate. Use off-site storage only if absolutely necessary, and manage it tightly. If it is out of control, fix it.

Some thought also needs to be given to visitors. They bring valuables, equipment, coats, all the stuff that employees bring. As with a fantastic washroom, it sends a strong signal to visitors of the positive, caring manner in which an organization treats its people. The same facilities should be available to visitors as for regular occupants.

The need for storage has reasserted itself. It is vital, low in cost and high in impact. It is a convenience factor that, when appropriately provided, can allow focus on the more central features of the workspace. Of all the small stuff, it is the most significant in letting the occupants of your workspace know that you have thought of them. It is easy to get it right, and just as easy to forget to think about it. There are no excuses for getting it wrong.

THE EPHEMERA

What is important to one person is rarely important to another. The 12 Elements are challengeable and often challenged, with appeals for relegation of some and the inclusion of others but, through repeated testing, they have held firm. The workplace factors that do not make it onto the list of Elements are by no means unimportant or lacking in value, but they fall into one of two categories: the 'possibles' – minority interests, even if they are gaining in popularity and find vocal support – and the 'probables' – things we may want to include but that are not vital to the cohesion and success of the workplace. They should all be evaluated and thought through at the Brief stage. The items below are a representative sample and by no means the entire list.

POSSIBLES

Specific **facilities for cyclists and motorcyclists** over and above showers and changing facilities for everyone (featured in the Wash Element) generate a lot of emotion. Cyclists tend to be a forceful lobby, born of having to battle daily with much larger and potentially deadly road-hogging objects. Facilities may include covered and secure parking, drying rooms, space for storing helmets and leathers, and repair workshops. Much depends on the location and the travel patterns of members of the organization, but support for green travel should be welcomed and invested in. Landlords have often banked their sustainability assessment points with the provision of racks and showers in the darkest recesses of the basement, and in many cases these are deemed sufficient.

Then there is the increasingly interesting consideration of facilities to allow **pets** at work. Sparked by co-working spaces where dogs are commonplace, more organizations are relaxing guidelines and restrictions on bringing animals into the workplace. Of course, it is usually dogs, because no one has quite understood the benefit of a bird-eating spider as a pet in the first instance, let alone as a positive contribution in the office. Allergies to pets are common, however, and so care needs to be taken. When the sneezing starts, Fido stays at home.

Workplace has, at the time of writing, come alive to the idea of **biophilia**, previously addressed specifically in the chapter on "Influence". It effectively consists of four strands: natural daylight, views towards natural settings, the use of natural materials, and interior planting. At the time of writing there is something of a race to the printers to claim leadership in the area as it forms a central theme of the wider wellbeing bandwagon. There is presently little rigorous research into its effects, beneficial or otherwise, despite many claims. Most of what has been said to date is covered by the Terrapin Bright Green consultancy in its published works.[59]

Most thinking around workplace biophilia features the Element of Daylight most strongly, and others are captured in the Elements of Sense and Control. In many respects, therefore, the Elemental Workplace supports a biophilic approach without overtly defining it as such. Planting and visual connectivity would invariably be high on the list of considerations, but biophilia in itself is too broad to effectively constitute an Element in itself. In many respects, conceptually it is similar to wellbeing, and therefore the Elemental Workplace can be considered to be a biophilic framework if so desired.

PROBABLES

Then there is the whole idea of **branding**, as it is often represented and applied. Expression was discussed as one of the six 'e's of what an amazing workplace can do for you, therefore it is important – but branding is a subset of expression, one component. The meaning in this respect relates to the overlay that is applied when the workspace is designed – vinyls, light boxes, three-dimensional installations and other such representations of the organization's identity. A delicate balance needs to be struck, but rarely is, between connecting the space, the organization and its people, and overdoing the whole exercise to the extent that it becomes counter- productive. The workplace has to 'feel like' it belongs to and is representative of the organization, but not as though a panic has erupted and people may suddenly forget who they work for. In the latter cases, branding spills over into billboarding, when the internal experience is akin to that a consumer or member of the public may feel externally. Internal workplace branding is not a sales exercise; it is another means by which loyalty can be created and an emotional connection made. It can be incredibly subtle and yet still be highly effective – or can be non-existent yet the workplace and the behaviours within still reflect the DNA of the organization.

Perhaps at last the idea of the **boardroom** may have had its day in the double-aspect sunshine. It is often

---

59 William Browning, Catherine Ryan and Joseph Clancy, *14 Patterns of Biophilic Design* (New York: Terrapin Bright Green LLC, 2014).
https://www.terrapinbrightgreen.com/report/14-patterns/

the most luxuriously furnished room in the building, with a table buffed with hair from a badger's backside, rectangularly set to articulate traditional power structures for the occasional attendance of a group who (with one or two exceptions) only work a few days a year for the organization. The more efficient and effective option is that the 'boardroom' can be any room, whenever it is called the boardroom. If the board use a room that the rest of the employees use, it may also help them understand a little more about the organization.

Very often the **reception** area absorbs considerable design time and focus. The speculative development guidebook has rather spoiled the welcome for millions, with its obligatory imposing "What the heck are you doing here?" monolithic desk, double-height space, large square of deep pile carpet and bank of bachelor- pad Barcelona chairs that appear too imposing to sit on – and, of course, stifling silence. It is preferable for reception areas to not actually look, operate or feel like a reception area. While still being a space at which you arrive, it can be a workspace, a café, a development zone – anything that is engaging and productive, an extension of the space beyond, presenting an almost seamless transition, secure but low-key. The project budget will breathe a sigh of relief, too.

When you need diagrammatic instructions to turn lights on and off, when you are presented with a choice of 16 different scene sets, or when you need to wave your arms around to tell the energy-conserving 'brain' that you are still in the room but not engaged in aerobic exercise, you know you have gone too far with the sustainability-points-accruing **lighting control system**. Automated sensory adjustment to daylight penetration is environmentally advisable. For the remainder, we welcome the humble, simple, binary bliss of a light switch. That and a sensible good-neighbourly approach to turning stuff on when you need it and off when you do not.

'Feature' anything can bring down a workplace budget all on its own – floors, lighting, ceilings or staircases – because 'feature' usually means taking out and discarding something that worked and replacing it with something much more expensive that adds no further functionality, and is usually much harder to maintain. It is a simply a flourish, an attention grabber, and possibly the iconic installation for which the workplace will be known. A better starting point is to work with what is there, making small and low-cost but intelligent and creative modifications.

Finally, there are the **Christmas socks:** the collection of embarrassing attempts to make claims to cultural lightness, originality and relevance such as Fussball tables, climbing walls, slides and meeting tables that double as table-tennis tables. The modern equivalent of the poster that says "You don't have to be mad to work here but it helps," they generally have an appeal that lasts as long as the dopamine rush. Such features can actually be inhibitors rather than enablers. When deciding whether to include such features, nine times out of ten do not, and on the tenth occasion think about them – then do not.

It is now useful to revert to how we create a fantastic workplace, armed with a better idea of each of the Elements and how they complement one another. I hope at this stage that you are convinced you can.

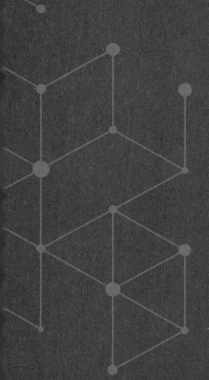

PART FOUR

HOW
(SECOND FIX)

RIVERS OF CHANGE

"You never step twice into the same river."
Heraclitus (cited in Plato, *Cratylus*, 402a)

JOURNEYS INTO CHANGE

'Change' is possibly the last frontier of workplace knowledge and practice, and one of the most difficult to obtain help with. There are no widely recognized qualifications available, established professional bodies speaking on its behalf, or reputable bodies of practitioners. Workplace change services are often offered by designers unable to disentangle themselves from their intended outcome, or consultants deflected from another path. The service is usually offered as 'change management', which in itself is an absurdity. It is possible to manage 'a' change, for example, from the use of one system or process to another. However, it is not possible to manage 'change' *per se*, as it is chaotic, unstructured, amorphous, and obeys neither law nor instruction. It has to be enabled, inspired, facilitated and cajoled. It is highly iterative, uncertain and insecure. Progress can be unravelled in a moment and giant steps can be taken on an inflexion. Change is a frustrating yet beautiful thing, if indeed it is a 'thing' at all. It presents an ontological problem. Change is not being, it is becoming. We have already been introduced to Heraclitus, the original and possibly only genuine change professional, his contribution most perfectly captured in the simple phrase, "All is flux". If everything is change, how can we untangle and understand it?

In the opening chapter, it was stated that all workplace journeys are in fact change journeys of which the creation of the workplace forms part. It is quite a terrifying flip of the established understanding of the order of things. The undue dominance of the idea of 'adoption' has been challenged – the forcing of a new situation or reality upon people, the compression of individual journeys into a compulsory route march (bring your own sturdy boots). It is with these two thoughts in mind that the remainder of this chapter turns some other established ideas about workplace change on their head.

A fundamental myth is that people do not like change. There are words for the fear of most things, and there is *cainotophobia* for the fear of newness. However, this afflicts a small number of people. If you consider your own life, it is characterized by a multitude of change ideas, thoughts and intentions. The momentum we give our lives is the energy we create from change. While we hope for some elements of our lives to remain static, even within those we consider minor refinements that would increase our levels of satisfaction. It is always fascinating when groups are asked about the quality of their workspace. Very few claim to have amazing workplaces, very few point to extremely poor space – but almost everyone is open to the idea that it could be better. They want some things to remain constant, which may be location, company, or ease of access to amenities – but there is always an imagined and hoped-for room for improvement. The static human does not exist.

We then need to consider the fundamental idea of change: the journey. Due to the finality of creating space which is then to be occupied simultaneously by groups of people, workplace change is usually considered a common journey – "We're all in this together." The media, activities, events and other punctuations are all designed to create adoption of a new way of living and working en masse.

Observed behaviour post-move is then aggregated to measure success (or otherwise). We cannot help but to roll things up.

This is also an organizational trait in many other respects, as we ascribe an existential quality to an organization or a team, rather than consider that they are fundamentally a collection of individual people. We still find it difficult to conceive of a collection of individual, highly personal journeys as just that; we instinctively amalgamate and then interpret a collective need and behaviour. Yet the change journey is unique and experiential. The line over which individuals are all expected to cross interrupts each journey at a different point, rather than a collective moment. Though there is a tendency to assume that a short period of time after the 'project' is complete the change focus can be stood down, it needs to continue, in a form, without end. This sends a powerful message to all participants that their individual journey will be respected, as it instantly removes the constricting pressure to comply with a given message by a given date. It frees the spirit, calms the nerves and makes the entire process lighter and more positive. Put the shoehorns down.

MODELS AND PLANS

The difficulty of enabling change often creates a need to plan activity against a reassuring structure to add a level of security amid the swirling uncertainty. It is therefore worth mentioning several models of change that are routinely applied to all manner of projects in business – mainly in order to set them aside.

When thinking of change models, most people instinctively turn to the 'grieving curve' created by Elisabeth Kübler-Ross in 1969,[60] following a study of terminally ill patients. The curve takes us through a number of phases of change: shock, denial, frustration, depression, experimentation, acceptance, integration. Though often criticized for its lack of supporting evidence, the model has been deeply ingrained in our thinking about change, and is routinely applied to all manner of projects within business. The penultimate stage – acceptance – is possibly the most dangerous of all in thinking about opportunity-oriented workplace change, as it signifies the most reluctant form of acquiescence within a suffocating view that all change is bad. It does not fit with an opportunity-oriented approach and is best left alone.

Also in common use are Kurt Lewin's mechanical three-stage model[61] (unfreeze, change, refreeze) from the 1940s and John Kotter's eight-step guide[62] from 1996. Lewin, a physicist, likened achieving change to working a block of ice into a different shape by melting it, remoulding and then refreezing it in the desired shape. This approach reflects the adoptive rather than adaptive view that has been questioned. Kotter's eight steps could almost be squeezed into Lewin's three stages, and though it contains some useful considerations it is still adoption and risk-oriented, talking of obstacles, resistance and threats.

That is not to say we do not need a plan, and we clearly do. Yet a change plan is not something to be held captive by. Possibly one of the best descriptions of what this means is set out in a paper by the Melbourne-based consultancy Anecdote entitled "Three Journeys",[63] which looks at change in relation to Lewis and Clark's exploration of the as-then unknown American west. The three journeys were the simple, end-to-end vision, the preparation, and the actual expedition, each characterized by the availability of richer information that enabled them to adapt, refocus and re-orient at each stage. The path they discovered was not that originally envisaged, yet it reached its destination. Our approach is, therefore, one of loose and iterative planning, not modelling.

AN EXPERIENTIAL FRAMEWORK

We open up the possibilities of the change journey in three broad ways. This is not a sequential or linear programme or even a change plan, but a guiding framework that will help as initiatives are devised and unfold. We generate an open, honest and informative dialogue that creates an emotional connection stimulating a desire to get involved and be part of the change. I am indebted to my colleague and friend Mark Tittle for his help in formulating this framework.

First, as a participant in the change, I am able to say that "**I know...**" – I am aware of what is happening and why, and what it means for me. I have received and understood information, and been able to ask questions and seek

60   Elisabeth Kübler-Ross, *On Death and Dying* (New York: Simon & Schuster/Touchstone, 1969).

61   Kurt Lewin, "Frontiers in Group Dynamics: Concept, Method and Reality in Social Science; Equilibrium and Social Change," *Human Relations*, Vol. 1, No. 5 (1947) p5–41.

62   John Kotter, *Leading Change* (Cambridge, MA: Harvard Business School Press, 1996).

63   Shawn Callahan and David Drake, "Three Journeys: A Narrative Approach to Successful Organizational Change," *Anecdote* (2007) http://www.anecdote.com/papers/Anecdote-3JourneystoChange_v1s.pdf

clarifications to make sure there is no doubt or uncertainty. Regrettably many change initiatives end here, and the results of this are felt much later.

When talking with people about the change, we should try to tell a story that they can relate to, so that it means something to them personally. Change stories can often be self-important and couched in terms and language that create distance. In this sense, taking time to think about the manner in which information will be conveyed – the lexicon and tone of voice – is important. The more down to earth and honest this is, the more it will resonate. Carefully crafted and edited corporate-speak using words and phrases that never pass our lips creates an instant divide, a feeling that something is being done to us rather than with us. The style also needs to be consistent, and so several people will have to master it so that it sounds as one voice. This will encourage people to speak positively about the change, and start to create a reinforcing narrative of their own.

Secondly, I am able to say that **"I feel..."** – I have an emotional connection, I am engaged, it means something to me and I am excited by what is to come (and may still be a little apprehensive too, but that is OK).

In creating an emotional connection and engaging people, we generate commitment. People feel part of the change, feel excited and supported. There may still be doubt and anxiety, but there is an inner confidence that this will be addressed and resolved. It is no longer just something being done that they have been asked to go along with, but something they are doing too. They want to join in, so that when involvement is requested they are happy to take part, whether that be attending an event or being part of a group creating something.

Many change initiatives unfortunately stop here, too, leaving the entire responsibility in the hands of the change and project team.

Third, I am able to say that **"I will do..."** – I am actually involved and am committing to some action; I am not a passive bystander waiting for something to be done to me. At this point responsibility becomes shared. Even a simple pyramid structure of steering group, change lead and move co-ordinator will ensure that approximately 7-10% of the workforce has a specific positive role to play.

Typically, a steering group will consist of a small number of senior people (albeit it would be interesting to make this a more dynamic cross-section of the organization) who set and remain closely associated with the vision, approve funding, are visibly associated with supporting the change and resolve any sticky issues. Change leads (sometimes called 'change champions') are usually fairly senior individuals representative of the business who collectively act as a manageably sized communication channel with colleagues, providing general business information to and receiving information from the project team, and able to take decisions on shared issues. Move co-ordinators, usually team administrators or people with local influence, are appointed later in the project, handling the detailed move information on behalf of their team and all practical move matters. As for scale, a workable rule of thumb would be a minimum of one member per 100 colleagues for the steering group, 1:50 for change leads and 1:25 for move co-ordinators.

There will usually be other opportunities to be involved, such as focus groups to develop certain areas of the Brief, or special interest groups responding to challenges around wellbeing or on-site amenities. It may be as simple as willingly attending events designed to inform. As the journey is personal to every person affected, being part of a collective positive change through taking personal responsibility for being prepared is incredibly powerful. A degree of gamification of the process can also help, where certain opportunities are opened to those who have completed several preparatory tasks. It also allows time for celebration of both the effort comprising the change and the impact.

(R)EVOLUTION?

When there is a desire to use the workplace as a catalyst for cultural change and to transform the working environment and style, how bold are you going to be? Are you going to reach straight for the endgame, bypassing several interim phases in a heroic revolution, or take it step by step, evolving carefully? There is no right or wrong strategy, but there are deep implications for the approach to change.

A single, bold leap allows the vision of the endgame to be fully painted, and enables the building of a prototype of the space and work settings that allows people to see, touch and learn about their new reality. It facilitates a more effective Brief process, since to be coherent it needs to be both broad and deep. It is likely to generate high levels of apprehension and excitement in equal measure, and in doing so can create a strong emotional connection, a togetherness on a bold mission despite the dangers and risks. It reassures too, in that after the leap is made, everything will settle quickly and the new environment can be enjoyed. It also allows the possibility of retreating slightly if the endgame is seen as too ambitious or too difficult to understand based on present circumstances. Yet there are likely to be significant risks, and the challenge of maintaining the togetherness over time as the faith is tested. It may be more difficult to persuade the sceptics to come on the journey. During the design process, the desire to reinvent everything can become contagious and needs to be handled carefully. In such a scenario, it is vital to ensure that what works in the existing space is retained, that there are links from the future back to the present to hold on to. There is also the risk that it may not work, or may be sabotaged (even unconsciously) along the way.

A series of planned incremental steps towards the vision, allowing it to evolve, can mitigate risk and provide reassurance. It can still create a sense of togetherness and help with building a deeper, more organic understanding of why the change is being made and what it means for everyone involved. It can be especially useful where no form of change in the workplace has occurred for many years. There is, however, the risk that if the plan looks too much like the present, some may question the need for change at all, and the change journey can potentially become more difficult as at each stage the occupants hammer the tent pegs in fully, only to be asked to rip them out again. Fatigue and confusion can set in and resistance develop, as the dreamscape appears increasingly distant. There is a risk that the vision will never be realized.

From both an outcome and a change perspective in a context-free 'laboratory' scenario, this book promotes a preference for taking one inspired step – revolution over evolution. Its potential as a vehicle for optimism, prototyping, stimulating the imagination and a sense of possibility, holds far greater potential. The risk is manageable if set up and performed well.

AVOIDING COMMON GOOFS

Enabling change is tough; things can go wrong. However, there are half a dozen things we can look out for that can help avoid self-inflicted problems.

First, **the small stuff matters**. Workplace change, like most major programmes, has a propensity to move from the macro to the micro while missing out many transitory phases. In one particularly radical change to a workplace observed, the most talked about issue, beyond the dramatically improved aesthetic and amenities, was that with teams sharing space it was difficult to find a stapler. For this reason, workplace design very much needs to "sweat the small stuff", yet so often does not. Very often the project team are looking through one end of their telescope and the occupants through the other end of theirs. As people move through their journey, they will come across items and ideas out of place. These items will come to symbolize the entire process of adjustment. Even tidying a room at home has the same effect. Rearranging the contents of the kitchen cupboards may create a much more logical cooking arrangement, but things are not where they used to be. When raised, the small stuff is not a cause for irritation but a clear sign that people are engaged. It is a good thing.

Secondly, **it's not a battle**. We have mentioned lexicon and tone of voice, but also of vital importance is how our choice of words reflects our stance. Fear can be sensed very easily. A risk-oriented approach can naturally lead to a contagious use of expressions within the team such as conflict, resistance and damage limitation. It leads to the positioning of certain issues based on likely opposition, thereby eroding engagement and participation. It is often thought that 'getting out in front' of issues that might be problematic is the best way to deal with them, but it can drive a strategy based on battling a collection of isolated concerns that might not actually be problems at all, hoping to minimize casualties. However, a consistently positive orientation can encourage people to consider outcomes for themselves rather than expecting to be gifted solutions that they can then critically evaluate and choose to reject. There will be enough amazing things about your scheme that can create this confidence; focus on them.

Thirdly, **listen**. The process of change must involve two-way communication. There is an incredibly tough balance to strike between taking down requirements and holding an effective conversation. To what extent is the process 'consultation' or 'engagement'? Very often individuals and teams will approach the transformation of the workplace using methods and terms that are familiar to them. People need to feel as though they have a voice and have been heard. This involves giving people the means and the permissions to express themselves, and providing a recognition that they have been heard. As we have established that the journey is personal, so too should be the conversation. Town halls are great for those with a voice like a foghorn and the confidence to use it, but not productive or useful for those with less of a propensity to speak openly, so they need a channel for a much more personal conversation. Feedback will contain wisdom and insight, and should be expected to, as there will be great ideas within strands of concern and clarification. A design exhibition, where the early-stage scheme design is set out for everyone to visit at their own time and for as long as they wish, with an opportunity to talk to the whole project team, is a super way to engage a large number of people, to create great conversations and for the team to learn. Active listening at events such as these allows the team to look for and act upon 'desire lines' – pathways people will naturally tread, regardless of where you were intending to build the path.

Fourth, **don't instruct, enable**. In the chapter "Scope: The Social Workplace", the patronizing horrors of etiquette and protocol training were first alluded to. It has unfortunately become routine when attempting to ensure adoption that a common approach is also taken to behaviours expected in the transformed workplace. Very often such instructions reinforce behaviours that are already commonplace, which can puzzle and confuse. The counter-argument hinges on the fact that we instinctively know what the appropriate behaviour looks like, and where we may have doubts the evidence around us from the behaviour of others points us in the right direction. An effective appeal in this regard is one of neighbourliness, as we have explored. It involves mutual respect and a shared interest in looking after our environment so that our colleagues can enjoy it too. The danger lies in over-prescription, which can create a corresponding tendency to rebel. If the design is effective, and whispers softly to us how to use the workspace for maximum benefit, we should not need to be instructed on how to use it: we will just know.

Fifth, **you are not alone**. Every workplace transformation is different. The change journey within which it sits will ebb and flow, snake back on itself, and enjoy moments of clarity and stasis in equal measure. If you have a responsibility for such a programme, it is worth acknowledging your vulnerability at the outset, and your willingness to revisit and revise the plan.

Do not assume and project a godlike status, or claim to be a psychological genius who understands people's every mood, whim and irrational concern. You will have your own journey to go on too, alongside and related to that of everyone else. You are not alone, so do not isolate yourself in the belief that you are. It is OK to have moments when you have no idea what to do, or why something has happened. Humans are incredibly resourceful; you will always find a way through it. A useful technique for this is to borrow the strength and confidence needed from your future self. Imagine a time long after the project is complete when you are relaxing, reflecting on a job well done, and recalling this time when you had no idea how you were going to solve the issue. You did, because you finished the job, and everyone loves their new workplace.

Lastly, **forget 100%**. There will be those for whom the change journey barely ever begins, either because they do not want it to, or simply because they do not grasp what it means. The latter can apply to highly intelligent and capable people, too. The fact is that no one ever remains at the starting gate. Even an awareness and rejection of the 'why' is a step. They should be given the same freedom as everyone else, but no more attention than anyone else. Attention is in some, but by no means all, cases the aim. The focus of the project team must always be consistent and fair. In time, when no one is looking, they will take the steps needed.

TUMMELING OUT

In an earlier chapter, we mentioned a term that for many is unfamiliar, that of *tummeling*. It is a Yiddish expression that originates from the German *tummeln*, which means "to stir". It is so underused that it even fails the spellcheck.

A tummeler is a person who catalyses others to action; one is traditionally designated at Jewish weddings to encourage everyone to dance. The term was first brought into usage in the digital workplace by Kevin Marks, Heather Gold and Deb Schultz in the USA and encapsulated in the website tummelvision.tv. It is a direct lift from the digital realm.

The term emerged during the search for an elusive magic dust. What turns a beautiful yet sterile workplace into a dynamic, pulsating, ever-transforming environment, heralded by an extensive and inclusive change programme? Lloyd Davis, who brought the idea to life in his role as Social Artist in Residence at the previously mentioned Centre for Creative Collaboration in London, described it in conversation as the active process of "doing things differently and talking about doing things differently". For a workplace to take on a life of its own, it needs the tummelers. They are not a hired band of experimentalists, they are people already within the organization, already at work in the space. They need to be given the freedom to do things differently, and their effect will be apparent. The first step is understanding that this is needed, the second is identifying the tummelers in your midst, and the third is creating the metaphorical space for them to operate. The essence of successful and lasting workplace change? Set people free.

WORKPLACE WELLBEING (REPRISE)

The goal of improving the wellbeing of building occupants is an incredibly powerful change tool. We mentioned, when discussing why we needed to create a fantastic workplace, that the Elemental Workplace is itself a framework for wellbeing, in that a number of the Elements create conditions beneficial to wellbeing in the workplace, while a number of others create the possibility of our making better choices and decisions. We can now segregate the Elements accordingly, and expand on that thinking.

If our **inclusive** workplace is flooded with natural **daylight**, if there is sufficient **space** with **comfortable** and ergonomic settings, if it is inspiring and stimulates the **senses** and our technology **connects** us seamlessly to the networks and highways we need, if we can use well-stocked and pleasant **washrooms** and **store** our stuff securely, then we are going to feel considerably more positive about our place of work, our colleagues and ourselves. Our physical condition and frame of mind are being looked after. It is playing to our wellbeing. We do not need to do anything, it is just happening for our benefit.

If we have the opportunity to **control** our environment, if we have a plentiful **choice** of settings to suit our every need that gets us up and mobile during the day, that in turn offers the potential for us to **influence** as required, and the opportunity to **refresh** with healthy food and drink, then we have a landscape in which we can exercise our judgement and make decisions that will benefit us. We can take a personal responsibility for our wellbeing, and have that enabled and respected by the organization. We may not always make the right call, but the potential exists. It is up to us.

Of course, there is a lot more to providing a balanced, comprehensive and coherent approach to workplace wellbeing in the areas of culture, process, management and amenities. However, every aspect of the Elemental Workplace can make a significant contribution to wellbeing, and therefore it creates an infrastructure on which to build the rest of the strategy. It provides a personal frame of reference for the changes about to unfold, and an anchor for individual aspirations.

BRINGING THE
WORKPLACE ALIVE

As we have established, workplace is a journey not a product, a perpetual beta trial. Its life is prolonged, made happy, given meaning and purpose through the service that is delivered to the occupants. From the initial greeting on entering the space to its maintenance, cleaning, security, catering and hospitality, health and safety, wellbeing services, technology and the notices on the walls, how you are welcomed and looked after in the workplace is just as significant as its form. A workplace transformation invariably requires a similar transformation of the service culture, however effective the present offering may seem. Very often this is a challenging proposition, as it could be that the bulk of the people presently delivering the service will be required to continue but to behave differently, and consistently so. Even within the most benign organization there often resides the belief among the service team that an underlying 'expectation culture' exists. This is a barrier to excellence that can be overcome with the shift described below.

In the early 1990s, when facilities management (FM), as it christened itself, was in its infancy as an idea and discipline, a number of practitioners who would regularly meet agreed that the day when airlines and hotels contacted FM organizations to ask how amazing-quality service is delivered would mark the day that FM had 'arrived'. The call has not been made. FM still lags behind as a service-oriented discipline. A principle drawback is that it is not selling directly to paying customers who exhibit any form of loyalty or advocacy, or can make a considered (or even impulsive) choice. Its recipients cannot decide who cleans their desks, preferring the quality or approach of one vendor over another. FM therefore has to try harder, and believe more deeply in its mission.

It could even be that, since the challenge was set, the practice of facility managers adopting the lexicon and mindset of 'customer service' has worked against them. Given their monopoly situation, it has placed them at a disadvantage. A different approach is required, one for which I owe the credit to Nick Green while he was Property Director at Sky in the UK. The organization has external customers for whom it provides products or services, or both. The FM team, meanwhile, are colleagues of those for whom they are providing a service within the organization. It is their task to make the working lives of their colleagues simpler and easier, and to make their experience of the working environment as positive as possible. A collegiate approach has the benefit of creating a mindset of being 'in it together', equal partners in supporting the mission of the organization. It removes the target – the symbol of an unequal relationship – from the back of the FM team. Most importantly, in adopting this approach it imposes a high level of responsibility to perform: FM cannot let their colleagues down.

A workplace can be made or broken by its service quality, a fundamentally operational activity. Keeping the lights on, maintaining buildings, ensuring workplaces remain inspiring, guaranteeing people and assets remain safe and secure, feeding people healthily, managing large operating costs responsibly – none of these functions are, or will ever be, strategic. They are not even tactical. Yet they make a significant, in many cases vital, and, in some instances, a business-critical contribution to an organization. Doing it damn well requires empathy, common sense, commitment, energy, and a hunger for better ways to do things, with occasional (usually accidental or expedient) innovation. It requires talking to people confidently like adults and equals, looking for opportunities (as opposed to order-taking), acting quickly and responsibly, doing what is promised, focusing on the detail and sweating the small stuff, taking pride in what has been achieved and using it as a baseline to improve further.

It is not about striving for a seat at the table, claiming strategic relevance or self-promotion – all of the usual stuff of conference sessions. Without effective service delivery, there *is* no table. Acknowledgement and respect will accrue throughout an organization to a confident and assured function happy in its contribution. There is nothing complicated in all of this, but it is clearly not easy because too few do it well. For most, there is still a long way to service excellence.

Little of this has anything to do with outsourcing. Whichever model is operated, service quality can be amazing – thereby justifying the procurement route – or a stale and disinterested service will prompt the opposite response. The entire industry oscillates between insourcing and outsourcing, yet manages to sustain a huge outsourcing industry at both the single-task level and in what is termed 'total facilities management' (TFM). It is quite possible to create a sparkling service under either approach or a hybrid; the debate is a distraction and often an excuse.

The FM industry also struggles with its asset-based approach. Though it has been common for FM suppliers to claim a people-centric, community-enablement approach, the commercial and business models under which they operate and are remunerated are almost exclusively still asset-based. Only when this changes will the industry have taken the significant step it articulates.

Workplace service excellence can be captured in three 'c's: competence, confidence and contribution.

It is an accident that they all begin with 'c'. **Competence**, because while the tasks are operational they are still in most cases vocational, and require the people performing them to know what they are doing and why. There are a host of regulations and laws governing service delivery, and knowledge needs to be current and thorough. "Operational" still means skilled – there is no such thing as unskilled work. **Confidence**, because the teams performing the services need to understand their part in the organization's success. In adapting to a mindset of equal partner with core business functions rather than struggling under the weight of an inferiority complex, service delivery teams feel capable and empowered. Finally, **contribution** – because there is not only no workplace without the service team, there is no organization or business. The contribution breeds pride and further reinforces competence. It creates careers and a desire to progress and grow. Trained, qualified people can confidently make a vital contribution to the collective success of the organization.

Yet there is one more factor to consider, which took many years to identify and still in many respects remains a mystery to service teams. That is **intensity**. High-quality service never lets up, never rests, never takes its eye off the smallest detail, never stops looking for ways to improve, never forgets a smile, never overlooks a chance to engage or update, never hides, always links to other services leaving no loopholes or vulnerabilities, always listens openly and with interest, respects every recipient of its offering, and always speaks with passion for its purpose. Fantastic service is delivered with a heightened state of emotional awareness. Creating and leading high-quality service teams is not easy – leaders need to embody the belief. Once achieved, their pressure on the pedal is required progressively less. But when the intensity drops, errors occur, and the task of rebuilding is incredibly difficult, for intensity is a fragile state. When you are able to sense that the intensity is right, it is a wonderful feeling.

Everyone deserves a fantastically serviced workplace. If a transformed workplace is not serviced fantastically, the effort, commitment and energy that brought it into being will be rapidly undone. The Elemental Workplace will ensure it is designed and created to enable it to be serviced easily and well. The service itself comes from competence, confidence and a keen sense of contribution, delivered with an intense focus on quality. There is room for an Elemental Service guide. The target is that phone call: "How do you *do* it so well?"

WHAT COULD POSSIBLY GO WRONG?

Listening to workplace case studies at conferences, you would be forgiven for thinking that nothing ever goes wrong. It would be doubtful whether these conference-presented studies would survive being delivered internally. The question, "What would you do differently?" is often the thinly veiled way of asking about the aspects no one likes to admit to. This is despite the growing recognition that we learn from failure, and that we 'work out loud' (for more on this, see the work of John Stepper[64]). We do not seem, however, to be able to openly and honestly 'fail out loud'.

Aside from our inhibition, one reason why you will not find a workplace scheme in the Museum of Failure in Helsingborg, Sweden, is that such projects rarely fail in total. Failure by degree, or in a more fractured manner, is far harder to pin down and is offset also by those aspects that are working. However, it is worth exploring some common reasons for failure, which may help us avoid some of the more cavernous pitfalls.

PEOPLE LEAVE, PEOPLE JOIN

Though it is not like building a medieval cathedral (Cologne in Germany took 632 years to complete), a workplace transformation can often have a 2-3 year life where new construction is concerned. A lot happens in this time. Projects do not always fall neatly into career timelines. Key team members rarely sign up to a captive assignment as though it were a mission to Mars. Their personal lives

---

64   John Stepper, *Working Out Loud* (New York: Ikigai Press, 2015).

and levels of focus will change too. Creating and maintaining a team balance and chemistry is a delicate art, and one vital to a successful outcome. The team carefully assembled on day one will not be the team that cuts the ribbon. As a rule of thumb, if the chemistry of a team does not feel right, it is not right. That is the only measure for an instinct. Throughout the project, as people leave and new people join, trust your instinct, every time.

NATURAL OBSOLESCENCE

Where technology and design are concerned, there is a natural lag in all but the most transient of projects. This is simply the result of the time it takes to propose a project, budget, commit, design, procure, build and occupy, from idea to finished product. For most major workplace projects, the ideas implemented and the technology in play are usually therefore somewhere between two and five years behind the day the space is occupied. Fortunately, as technology becomes more mobile and cloud-based, other than the creation of the best possible connectivity, the lag is shortening slightly. However, what is in our heads now, and what we dreamscape, is generally years away. As much as possible should be left to a just-in-time design and procurement approach, and the firm acknowledgement of workplace as perpetual beta should allow for catch-up post-completion.

MONEY COMES, MONEY GOES

Working with tiny budgets can be incredibly satisfying – design has to be more intelligent, the limited pot of cash managed more astutely, and there is often a far greater sense of pride associated with an amazing outcome from a proportionally small investment. A project with an eye-watering budget and an army of consultants is just as likely to fail as one on a fraying shoestring; money guarantees nothing. Yet the problem comes when the budget is cut midstream, when the Brief and early design work on which everyone is engaged cannot be delivered. This is not a new thing: Beaumaris Castle in Wales went over budget in 1296 and was never finished.

It is always worth working on a simple structure throughout the project, identifying essentials, should-haves and would-like-to-haves. This three-way analysis of every component enables a drop-back at any point in time to a lower cost base, without a considerable amount of arm-waving or redesign. It is a simple, effective and mature discipline, and allows an option-based approach from the outset.

TANGENTS BECOME FRESH TRACKS

The briefing, design and creative process is never linear, despite its arrangement in a sophisticated model complete with critical paths and vital dependencies. The exploration of ideas, possibilities, and opportunities throughout this process is vital – that is, until the tangent becomes a parallel or divergent path, and you cannot get back onto the original track. You may not realize this for some time, since the tasks look surprisingly similar. The outcome however will look very different. Remaining true to the vision, the "why?" and the intended outcome is a vital part of the project, despite temptations dropped intentionally and accidentally into the path.

"BUILD IT AND THEY WILL COME"

While by creating a new workplace you logically increase the odds of positive behaviour change, by the same token, by creating the workplace and not manifesting the idea – as by not engaging with its occupants – you decrease the possibility of its success in beneficially changing behaviour. On your travels and in your research, you will discover amazing physical spaces that just do not work, because the creators believed that was enough. It is never enough. Change needs to be nurtured, enabled, facilitated, continued. Build it and you will just have built it, nothing more. They will likely go somewhere else.

THE LURE OF 'COOL'

It was assumed at the very beginning of the book that workplace environments are created for people, and the question was asked how they could possibly be created for anything else. The potential issue is that the physical form of the workplace, the statement it makes, even potentially the dominance of one of the six 'e's (such as expression or environment) is given prominence, and the excitement of creating a space that challenges norms and expectations takes control. One of the most recent forms of this is the dominance and lure of the idea of 'cool'. As an aspiration and potential outcome, it is everywhere that workplace professionals tread.

We can be forgiven at times for thinking we are being bombarded with effortless nonchalance. A clutch of websites such as *Fast Company*, *Forbes* and *Inc.* frequently parade the "coolest workplaces in the world", photographed prior to occupation – they make superb, glossy clickbait after all. This is because invariably it is about the aesthetic. These envy-inducing displays overlook the fact that a space looks a lot different when actually occupied. Also, a workplace may be deemed to be cool due to the attitude and behaviours of the occupants or the nature of the undertaking, which may have nothing to do with how it looks. It is a very personal thing, too – what is cool to one person is often not to another.

The workplace has to work, and to do so sometimes it is not 'cool', but just works. Great design and an inclusive, comfortable aesthetic are appreciated, but the style and form of the outcome should not be permitted to become a narcissistic end in itself. Cool may be a by-product if you wish it to be, but try not to make it an aim.

HIDDEN FORCES

Throughout the creation of a fantastic workplace, we will have forces working on our behalf, and several working against us. An awareness of what they are will help, as we will need to manage their impact. In some cases, they are a two-sided coin. A lot more could be said about each, but here is a brief run-through.

FORCES WORKING FOR US

What we might call **Googleization** has created a far greater awareness of the possibilities of workplace than at any previous time. The growth of co-working spaces, where effective design generates business, has built on this. You can do what you want – things no longer have to be grey or beige – but caution is needed with the toys.

Instant accountability, as many brands have discovered the hard way, has created far less tolerance of poor quality and negation of responsibility than ever before, as there is no longer any hiding place. The provision of a poor workplace will be talked about, and photos shared, relentlessly. People are surprisingly open and carefree with the share-free. Of course, this could work against us too if things start to go wrong, so handle with care.

Inevitably, **technology**, when used appropriately, holds a massive potential to improve our lives and set us free (and, on the downside, enslave us – be careful of this too), much of which has yet to be realized despite commentary to the contrary. We are still in the throes of mimicking existing practice with technology; there is so much more to come as we dispense with old metaphors and create new. Antony Slumbers captures this succinctly with his phrase "Don't digitise the past."[65]

Connectivity through social tools has created a capacity to discover, befriend and share with people that physical networking could never have made possible. That is, as long as we embrace the 'gift economy' of social media, leave our crumpled texts of *The Art of War* in the management development seminar, and ignore the trolls.

The trend towards **globalization**, despite its recent setbacks (which are surely temporary), has provided greater access to, and knowledge and insight into, differing ways and approaches than ever before. The days of the 'global [parent country] workplace standard' are almost over, thankfully. Even the big banks are recognizing this.

Design itself has a massive potential to create and shape culture. It is a fascinating idea that physically speaking 'culture' does not exist, that there is just an *idea of culture* formed under historical conditions[66] that paves the way for the contribution design is able to make. It can, however, just as easily be applied badly and cement a rotten culture. Never underestimate the power of design. It breakfasts with culture and picks up the tab.

The growing interest in **workplace as a discipline**, not just from its ugly sibling, real estate, but from other sectors, is moulding the idea of workplace as a body of thought, skill and practice that can create amazing outcomes. It will draw the disparate threads of design, consulting, strategy and academia together. Expect this to grow rapidly and eventually consume FM before seeking other snacks.

It no longer depends on chance. **Evidence** is mounting, and easily available. Whether through data and story collection or the critical mass of successful schemes, there are no longer any excuses for not being able to simply and easily source meaningful and practical inspiration and justification, with a little time and application and comparatively little expense. This has also (fortunately) changed the role of consultants in the field (should they choose to heed it) from purveyors of mystical remedies to curators of inspiration. Snake oil is still available in a variety of sizes, though.

Finally, there is an increased awareness of the importance of **people-centricity**, whereby people come before the asset. The 85/10/5 split in costs discussed earlier in this book, only a few years ago a mystery, is now regularly quoted. Offering such a people-centric view no longer marks you out as an irresponsible crank – you are on the money.

FORCES WORKING AGAINST US

Deep in the infrastructure lies the pervading **management culture** – behaviours such as panoptic management are often embedded in organizational culture, but also in our education and practice, having delivered the prosperity of our age. It is easy to lay the blame on Taylorism, but many supposed modern alternatives are built on the same productivity metaphor. A workplace scheme, floating in the superstructure, will never solve 100 years of common practice on its own.

Gadgetization, or technology for technology's sake, works against itself through sucking in time, energy,

65 Antony Slumbers, "You Need a Digital Strategy", *Innovation in Real Estate*, March 27, 2017 https://www.antonyslumbers.com/theblog/2017/3/27/you-need-a-digital-strategy

66 Son Mitchell, "There's No Such Thing as Culture: Towards a Reconceptualization of the Idea of Culture in Geography", *Transactions of the Institute of British Geographers*, Vol. 20 No. 1 (1995) p102-116.

resources, focus and motivation, the possibility of any gains obscured by its glow. Not every challenge has a technological solution. Sometimes the old ways of working still work.

Misguided ideals, such as the vanity of 'cool' previously identified, can trivialize the workplace, and focus attention not on the contribution it is making to people's lives, but on itself. Remove the mirror on the wall, should it appear.

Generationalism, as in making empty and unsupported assumptions about what 'younger people' want, drives a strategy agenda on thin air. The focus on the emerging workforce is having a detrimental impact on the needs of ageing contributors, who are growing in number and likely to be working longer. Colleagues in their later years are vital to those new to the workforce who have much to learn.

Silos, aka vested interests – which can be groups or individuals with mass, embedded status or a will to power, wanting to do something different or just not wanting to do what you do – can kill your case if it does not fit their plan. Know the silos, how they work and what they want. Ranting about silos does not break them down; talking to people can.

Compromise is an equal and opposite danger to that posed by silos. A project will have many competing demands, and the tendency is to try to satisfy everyone with a recognizable contribution and hence create a fruit salad of a mess. The role of the intelligent client is to weigh the importance of each interest and ensure that the project remains true to its aims and vision.

Over-complication or prevarication as a reason not to do anything is all too depressingly common and has been an underlying driver for the creation of the Elemental Workplace. Filibusters are everywhere.

Gimmickification occurs when people fixate on the lure of gaudy kindergarten treats that erode brain enamel until you end up with slides, climbing walls, deckchairs, hammocks and a gazebo, and your credibility in tatters. Really, if you have a gazebo, you have gone too far.

Mythification, or the perpetuation of our own vacuous hype – be it to do with collaboration, millennials, smart working, crazy spaces for crazy thinking, trust crises or, worst of all, 'this era of unprecedented change' – can create the wrong challenge and the wrong outcome. Though these ideas appear to support a case, their lack of substance merely undermines.

Bureaucracy, whether it be from the unconscious layering of policies and processes, the involvement of staff representative bodies, an inherently risk-averse organizational model, an approval process with more layers than a *mille-feuille,* or obfuscation as a means of control, can make it appear that the cuffs are applied just as the demonstration of the fine art of juggling is to begin. This is why Lockheed Martin set up its Skunk Works programme as long ago as 1943 to set small creative teams free of red tape to innovate unimpeded – but it is also why so few followed until recently (thinking it was a new idea).

Once we know what is working for us and against us, we can be ready to face the challenge.

PART FIVE

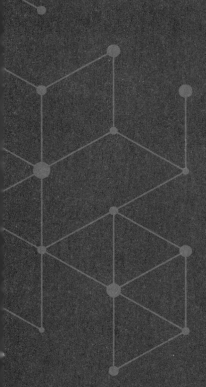

RESOURCES

THE ELEMENTAL
STANDARD

We have national and international standards in construction: BREEAM, LEED and more recently the WELL Building Standard. Each of these requires a team of consultants, lots of clipboards, a complex assessment methodology, extensive measurements for which few people understand the need or the outcome, and a large invoice at the end of the trial. While these are dressed up as people-focused standards, they are also still ultimately applicable to the built asset: the building gets the badge. Having set out a clear and simple approach to workplace design, it seems natural to offer a self-assessment tool for you to evaluate your own workplace. It may be useful in making the case, or in seeing how you fared when the project is complete, or both. No consultants are needed, no badges are awarded but, in taking a fair approach and being honest with yourself, you can award yourself marks and claim approval. You could even make your own badge.

The highest award is Elemental – as in attainable and expected, rather than a mark of exception and distinction, a matter of right. There is no reference to productivity; it is just assumed that if the workplace is decent, you will be able to get on with your work and will feel more valued, which must have a positive bearing on your contribution.

Some of the criteria and assessment measures could become unwieldy as a result of being debated and sub-divided, so there is a need here to exercise your own judgement in each case.

Each Element is assessed independently and then a score is obtained at the end – simple stuff.

DAYLIGHT

As much of it as possible, from as many angles as possible. There is no artificial source of this gift that comes close to that which pours plentifully from the sky. The measures applied here are self-explanatory.

Points	Condition
10	You are 20 large paces or less from a source of natural daylight in the place(s) you normally work for over half of the working day
5	You are 40 large paces or less from a source of natural daylight in the place(s) you normally work for over half of the working day
0	You work predominantly (over half of the working day) under artificial light only
-5	You work predominantly (over half of the working day) under artificial light, and it is under-powered for your needs, flickers, is a sickly yellow or is unreliable and gives you a headache

CONNECTIVITY

A wifi/network that works and kit that is sized and specified for your work. This one attracts extra points – it is the thing that needs fixing first, every time. It should be the first line on any workplace cost plan. We can operate effectively in a poor workplace with excellent IT and connectivity, as we do in less than ergonomic, noisy and insecure public spaces such as cafés, yet not the other way around. BYOD is seen here as a negative – it is yours, you should not have to use it for work (unless you are a freelancer or it is your business).

Points	Condition
15	Your ultralight laptop fits in your bag, does not prompt a call to the chiropractor at the end of each day, and has a flash drive and all of its keys, and the reliable data signal works just as well on Ethernet or wifi wherever you go in the building
10	All of the above, but your laptop is over two years old and everything works better when it's plugged into the Ethernet
0	Your laptop is a dog, has keys missing, and the network drops out like a 1960s art school hippy
-5	You have to rely on your own device because what you are given is a dog with keys missing – and you get your best connectivity at home

SPACE

Enough space to swing a toy cat? There has to be a threshold. On an overall net internal area basis, dividing our total space by the number of people working from it (subtle difference from the number working in it), the average should not go below 6m² (65ft²) per person. While there is probably an upper threshold too, such that we might be rattling around inside a vast expanse of office and not see a living soul for hours, that is unlikely to happen in this cost-conscious age. However, a bonus zero has been added for good measure, just in case. You don't need to physically measure it – just imagine yourself swinging a large toy cat and take a guess from there. You could always ask your facilities manager if you want the actual data.

Points	Condition
10	10-15m²/person
5	6-10m²/person
0	Less than 6m²/person
0	More than 15m²/person

CHOICE

You don't need the full catalogue of over-designed adolescent dens with infantile names, but you do need four basic types:

- Somewhere to work at a desk (or similar) with your team – a space that most would recognize as a standard desk in generally open space – let's call this 'primary' space
- Somewhere quiet and comfortable to focus alone (and it doesn't need the acoustic privacy of a padded cell to qualify), where people will leave you to get on with it
- Somewhere informal to meet with colleagues, write stuff up on a wall and leave it there
- Somewhere a bit more formal to meet, with a door (because not everything is good for everyone to overhear).

Let us call them the 'four key spaces' for now. It is all very well having a choice of physical spaces available, but you also need to be free to exercise those choices – so the scoring tries to take this into account too.

Points	Condition
15	You have access to the four key work settings, and are free to exercise a choice of what space you use and when
10	You have access to three or more of the four key work settings including primary, and are free to exercise a choice of what space you use and when
5	You have access to three or more of the four key work settings including primary, but need to get the OK to use anything other than primary
0	Primary and meeting rooms only, the booking of which is like trying to get a table at the Ivy – and you are expected to be seen at your desk unless you are in a meeting

INFLUENCE

Often miscued as 'personalization', this could mean that you exercise influence as a group or just you, it could mean just for the day or for longer. As long as you have some way of adding something so you create a bond with your space, however small.

Points	Condition
10	You can influence the space in which you work – you can move things around, leave your stuff out (taking care to make sure surfaces can be cleaned) and put your work on display on walls and whiteboards and leave it there
5	You can partially influence the space in which you work – you can leave your stuff out but have to clear surfaces at the end of the day, and put your work on display on walls and whiteboards during the day but clear it away at the end
0	The rules have been written by the secret police and anything you place or leave on the desk is destroyed overnight in a controlled explosion

CONTROL

This includes thermal comfort (temperature, humidity, air velocity and radiant temperature) and noise. The environment certainly does not have to be air-conditioned, but you do need to be able to vary the environmental conditions in response both to external conditions and to equipment, people and technology in the space.

Points	Condition
10	You can control some/all of these elements – particularly temperature – in the localized area in which you normally work (or can call someone to do it fairly quickly for you) and you have somewhere you can work that is quiet and free of distractions when you need it
5	You can control some/all of these elements – particularly temperature – in a large, open-space area in which you normally work (or can call someone to do it fairly quickly for you) and you have somewhere fairly quite and distraction-free you can work when you need it
0	You cannot control the temperature, humidity or draughts at all – you are stuck with the way it is – bring your own singlet or duvet, as appropriate and you are at the mercy of the varying din and distraction of your colleagues, with no escape

REFRESH

This refers to access to drinks and food, creating at least the potential for reasonable quality. This can be tricky to assess because there are no guidelines (formal or informal – ask anyone, get a different response) as to when a staffed facility should be provided within a building, given location and size factors, or the degree of subsidy that should be applied. The spectrum starts from a bare minimum of needing to have a clean, functional space for drinks and food to be prepared by the occupants. An entirely arbitrary divide has been created with two options, and food and drink have been gathered into a single category for our purposes. It is up to you which you choose to use.

If your workplace is either out of town (nothing decent nearby) and/or has more than 200 people wherever it is sited, it is assumed to have a staffed facility:

Points	Condition
10	You can obtain healthy food options, hot and cold, and high-street standard barista coffee at subsidized prices without leaving the building
5	You can obtain reasonably healthy food options, hot (if possible) and cold (at least), and bean-to-cup coffee at reasonable prices (as in, no higher than the high street) without leaving the building
0	It's powdered vend only (if that) or whatever you supply, and a trip down the high street for a very expensive sandwich

If your workplace is either in a city centre or an amenity-rich environment, or has fewer than 200 people, it is assumed *not* to have a staffed facility:

Points	Condition
10	You have a clean and well-maintained kitchen and food preparation area shared by fewer than 100 people, ample refrigeration and microwave ovens, tea and coffee is free and you have somewhere locally away from the desk to sit and consume your creations
5	You have a reasonably well looked after kitchen and food preparation area shared by fewer than 250 people, some refrigeration and a microwave oven, tea and coffee is free and you have somewhere locally away from the desk to sit and consume your creations
0	You have a furry kettle and a rusty teaspoon on a string, and you can only take your health-hazard of a drink back to your desk

SENSE

If you check the cover of Pink Floyd's *Dark Side of the Moon*, there is a whole colour spectrum out there. It changes our mood, lightens our spirit. The workplace should feel nice because we are allowed to touch it, and also smell nice too. Of course, 'nice' means different things to different people, but we generally all know what 'unpleasant' smells like.

Points	Condition
10	The workspace includes a variety of tastefully coloured and textured complementary finishes that provide interest and vibrancy, and the place smells nice
5	The workspace includes a variety of colours and textures, where someone has tried their best to make the place stimulating, and it smells either nice or neutral
0	Everything is beige on beige, flat on flat, all the way down, and it smells stale at best

COMFORT

You would like your spinal column to be intact at the end of the day, and your whole body to feel acknowledged and looked after while at work.

Points	Condition
10	Every setting feels intuative, welcoming, supports your physical needs and allows you to alter it to make it more appropriate to you
5	Settings are generally human-oriented, but there is a lack of control, meaning you need to use them as the designer thought best
0	Your work settings seem to have all appeared from the garden shed, and scream "get off me!" every time you make an approach

INCLUSION

Absolutely everyone deserves a fantastic workplace: it offers a home to everyone, where no one has to raise a particular need because it has already been fully thought through.

Points	Condition
10	The workplace appears to cater for everyone and anyone, it is well thought through, welcoming, accommodating and comfortable, with helpful and appropriate amenities
5	The obvious things appear to have been thought about, such as physical disabilities and gender, but thereafter it is variable
0	The workplace has been designed with the most basic needs in mind and does not consider any additional requirements

WASH

Facilities that are clean, warm, have hot water and soap, allow you to dry your hands on something unique to you, and have somewhere to hang up your coat and bag while you use them.

Points	Condition
10	The facilities are warm, clean and well stocked, and you generally have access to them when you need them (which is quite important with toilets)
5	The facilities are fairly warm, clean and well stocked, there are hooks for your stuff, and you generally have access to them when you need them – but it all could be improved
0	The facilities are cold, less than clean and invariably unstocked, and often in use by someone who seems to have fallen into a coma
-5	If a visitor has commented on the poor state of your facilities, a deduction for the shame of it

STORAGE

You need a place to put your stuff, with a lock on it. Your papers, your purse/wallet, your gym bag, maybe your shoes. And you would really like to trust that your stuff will be where you left it when you go to collect it.

Points	Condition
10	You have sole use of a locker or cupboard (or both) that can take a small gym bag, a pair of shoes, your laptop and some other stuff – and it is lockable
5	You share a storage facility for your stuff with one or two other people and it is lockable
0	You either do not have enough storage space for your stuff or it is not lockable – or both

ADD UP YOUR SCORE

This will range from a maximum of 130 to a minimum of -15. An Elemental Workplace cannot score any zeros. Here is the ranking:

Points	Ranking	Assessment
100+ (no 0s)	Elemental	Your workplace is amazing. Tell your friends, tell your Mum, tell everyone, and enjoy it – you are valued! You need a badge.
70-99	Decent	Not a bad place to work. But do watch out for where you hit some zeros – you may want to raise them with someone with a budget or a conscience. You need to give them a nudge.
30-69	Poor	It's not looking too good, is it? There are probably a few things that are OK, as you have a few points on the board. Still, some significant room for improvement. You need a plan.
1-29	Terrible	Crikey, your workplace is crap. Unless it's an amazing job and you work with fantastic people, you might want to re-evaluate why you are still there. You need a miracle.
0 or less	Shocking	You may wish to check that you are not working on the set of a sit-com, and then retake the survey to see if you cannot at least create a positive score.

All the Elemental ratings in each category are possible, with a little thought, some willpower, a recognition of the difference it will make to people, and a little cash. If we could do enough for every workplace to be Elemental, just imagine what we could achieve after that.

FURTHER READING

In addition to the books and papers referenced in the footnotes, here is a suggested reading list to enable you to follow any of the ideas or themes within the book. It is a potted, personal selection. There are of course many more – but this may just help get you started on what will inevitably be a never-ending trek. And, of course, there is nothing wrong with that.

BOOKS: WORKPLACE-ISH

Chang, Ha-Joon. *23 Things They Don't Tell You About Capitalism*. London: Penguin, 2011.

Clements-Croome, Derek (ed.). *Creating the Productive Workplace*. Abingdon: Routledge, 2018.

Coleman, Nathaniel. *Lefebvre for Architects*. Abingdon: Routledge, 2015.

Coplin, Dave. *Business Reimagined*. Petersfield: Harriman House, 2013.

Duffy, Francis. *Work and the City*. London: Black Dog, 2008.

Groves, Kursty and Knight, Will. *I Wish I Worked There!* Hoboken, NJ: John Wiley & Sons, 2010.

McEwan, Anne Marie. *Smartworking*. Farnham: Routledge, 2013.

Milligan, Andy and Smith, Sharon (eds.). *Uncommon Practice*. Harlow: Pearson, 2002.

Oldenburg, Ray. *The Great Good Place*. New York: Marlowe & Company, 1989.

Semler, Ricardo. *Maverick! The Success Story Behind the World's Most Unusual Workplace*. New York: Random House, 1993.

BOOKS: CHANGE

Berg, Insoo Kim and Szabó, Peter. *Brief Coaching for Lasting Solutions*. New York: Norton, 2005.

Callahan, Shawn. *Putting Stories to Work.* Melbourne: Pepperberg Press, 2016.

Dehnugara, Khurshed. *Flawed but Willing*. London: LID, 2014.

Jackson, Paul Z and McKergow, Mark. *The Solutions Focus.* London: Nicholas Brealey International, 2007.

BOOKS: PEOPLE

Berkun, Scott. *The Year Without Pants*. London: John Wiley & Sons, 2014.

Cederström, Carl and Fleming, Peter. *Dead Man Working.* Winchester: Zero Books, 2012.

Pessoa, Fernando. *The Book of Disquiet.* London: Serpent's Tail, 1991.

Pontefract, Dan . *Flat Army*. Hoboken, NJ: Jossey-Bass, 2013.

Semple, Euan. *Organizations Don't Tweet, People Do.* London: John Wiley & Sons, 2012.

Swann, Andy. *The Human Workplace.* London: Kogan Page, 2017.

Thoreau, Henry David. *Walden; or, Life in the Woods.* Boston: Ticknor and Fields, 1854.

Timms, Perry. *Transformational HR.* London: Kogan Page, 2017.

Ward, Colin. *Anarchy in Action.* London: George Allen & Unwin, 1973.

BOOKS: FICTION

Currell Brown, Peter. *Smallcreep's Day.*
   London: Victor Gollancz, 1965.
Melville, Herman. *The Piazza Tales.*
   New York: Dix & Edwards, 1856.

INDUSTRY REPORTS

The following are available as free downloads, the source of which can be traced using a suitable internet search engine:

100 Urban Trends: A Glossary of Ideas from the BMW Guggenheim Lab Berlin (Curated by Maria Nicanor, BMW Guggenheim Lab, and Amara Antilla, Curatorial Assistant, BMW Guggenheim Lab, 2012).
Building Productivity in the UK (ACAS Strategy Unit, 2015).
Growing the Health & Wellbeing Agenda (CIPD Policy Report, 2016).
Healthy Workplaces: A Model for Action (World Health Organization, 2010).
The Future of Work (Dept. of Trade and Industry (UK), 2006).
The Impact of Office Design on Business Performance (Commission for Architecture and the Built Environment and the British Council for Offices, 2005).
These Four Walls: The Real British Office (Gensler, 2015).
The Six Factors of Knowledge Worker Productivity (Advanced Workplaces Associates, 2015).
UK Workplace Survey (Gensler, 2016).
Workplace Strategies that Enhance Human Performance, Health and Wellness (HOK, 2013).

Working Without Walls: An Insight into the Transforming Government Workplace (Office of Government Commerce (London), 2004).

ARTICLES AND PAPERS

GENERAL WORKPLACE
Ellison, Ian. "Is This the Missing Piece of the Great Workplace Conundrum?" *Work&Place*. No.7 (2016): p8-1.1

Mau, Bruce. "An Incomplete Manifesto for Growth" (1998). http://www.manifestoproject.it/bruce-mau/

Sailer, Kerstin, Ros Pomeroy, and Rosie Haslem. "Ten Demonstrable Truths About the Workplace You May Not Know." *Workplace Insight* (2016). http://workplaceinsight.net/ten-demonstrable-truths-about-the-workplace-you-may-not-know/

PRODUCTIVITY
Oseland, Nigel and Adrian Burton. "Building a Business Case." *Facilities Management* (2013). http://www.workplaceun-limited.com/2013%20FM%20Business%20Case.pdf

DAYLIGHT
Joseph, Anjali. "The Impact of Light on Outcomes in Health Care Settings." *Centre for Health Design* (2006). https://www.healthdesign.org/sites/default/files/CHD_Issue_Paper2.pdf

Stevens, Richard G. and Yong Zhu. "Electric Light, Particularly at Night, Disrupts Human Circadian Rhythmicity: Is that a Problem?" *Philosophical Transactions of The Royal Society B* (2015). http://rstb.royalsocietypublishing.org/content/370/1667/20140120

SPACE

Sailer, Kerstin. "Creativity as Social and Spatial Process." *Facilities*, Vol. 29 No. 1/2 (2011): p6-18.

INFLUENCE

University of Exeter. "Designing Your Own Workspace Improves Health, Happiness and Productivity." *University of Exeter News and Events* (2010). http://www.exeter.ac.uk/news/featurednews/ title_98638_en.html

CONTROL

Leaman, Adrian and Bill Bordass. "Productivity: The Killer Variables." *Building Services Journal* (1998). http://www.usablebuildings.co.uk/Probe/ProbePDFs/ Probe15.pdf
Oseland, Nigel and Paige Hodsman. "Planning for Psycho-acoustics." *Workplace Unlimited Research Report* (2015). http://workplaceunlimited.com/Ecophon%20 Psychoacoustics%20v4.5.pdf

SENSE

Schliemann, Udo. "The Importance of Colour in the Work-place." *Work Design Magazine* (2017). https://workdesign.com/2017/04/importance-color-workplace/

COMFORT

Ergonomics and Human Factors at Work. London: Health & Safety Executive, 2013.
Home Sweet Office: Comfort in the Workplace. Zeeland, MI: Herman Miller, 2008.

INCLUSION

Aiden, Hardeep and Andrea McCarthy. "Current Attitudes Towards Disabled People." *Scope* (2014).

Fletcher, Howard. *The Principles of Inclusive Design.* London: Commission for Architecture and the Built Environment, 2006.

Oseland, Nigel. "The Impact of Psychological Needs on Office Design." *Journal of Corporate Real Estate* Vol. 11 No. 4 (2009): p244-254.

BLOGS

The following sites feature regular work, workplace and people-related insights:

Flip Chart Fairy Tales, https://flipchartfairytales.wordpress.com/
WORKTECH Academy, http://www.worktechacademy.com/about-worktech-academy/
Workplace Insight, http://workplaceinsight.net/
Dale, Gemma. *People Stuff,* https://hrgemblog.com/
Dryborough, Julie. *Fuchsia Blue,* https://fuchsiablueblog.wordpress.com/
Heath, Simon. *Murmuration,* https://workmusing.wordpress.com/about/
Morrison, Neil. *Change-Effect,* https://change-effect.com/
Sailer, Kerstin. *Spaceandorganization,* https://spaceandorganization.org/
Oseland, Nigel. *Workplace Unlimited,* http://workplaceunlimited.blogspot.co.uk/
Usher, Neil. *workessence,* http://workessence.com/

JOURNALS & MAGAZINES

FMJ – facility management and workplace issues

FX – workplace design, featuring recent schemes and current issues

Icon – workplace design and architecture

Journal of Corporate Real Estate – an academic journal exploring property and workplace issues

Mix Interiors – workplace design, featuring recent schemes and current issues

OnOffice – workplace design, featuring recent schemes, with analytical regular columns

Work&Place (online only, via *Workplace Insight*) – an almost-academic journal exploring work-related issues as they affect workplace design

ABOUT THE
AUTHOR

NEIL USHER

For more than 25 years in the property profession, Neil has been there and done it (strategy, development, transactions, workplace creation, change programmes, capital projects, operational management) at scale for a host of large and diverse organizations. The common theme in each case; organizations with a desire to transform their workplace, in need of the vision, plan and creativity to make it happen. From a blank piece of paper, he has created amazing people-centric workplaces across the globe, in Australia, Singapore, America, Canada, South Africa and Europe. Most recently he completed a multiple-award-winning workplace in West London, one of the world's largest, most progressive and amenity-rich agile environments. In 2011 he started writing a highly influential blog, workessence, which recently gave its name to his executive consulting business, and can be found on Twitter **@workessence**. He is a regular conference and academic speaker, and occasional performance poet. He lives in London with his family.

ABOUT THE ILLUSTRATOR

SIMON HEATH

Following a successful corporate career in senior operational management roles in financial services and workplace strategy, Simon now works in a consulting capacity with some of the world's leading brands, using his skills as an artist and communicator to help them navigate complex organisational challenges. He has a popular and irreverent blog where he writes on a host of workplace topics and authors the occasional article for more grown-up publications. He is an in-demand illustrator on the conference circuit and sometimes gets asked to speak at events. Sometimes he even says yes. He doesn't do suits. You can most commonly find him on Twitter where he is known as **@SimonHeath1**. In real life, he lives in Surrey with his wife, Jackie and their two awesome kids, Evie and Jack.

Everyone deserves a fantastic workplace.
Good luck with creating yours.